# LAND OF URBAN PROMISE

*Washington, D.C.*

# LAND OF
# URBAN PROMISE

## CONTINUING THE
## GREAT TRADITION

*A Search for Significant Urban Space
in the Urbanized Northeast*

by JULIAN EUGENE KULSKI

UNIVERSITY OF NOTRE DAME PRESS   1967
*Notre Dame      London*

COPYRIGHT © 1967 BY
UNIVERSITY OF NOTRE DAME PRESS
NOTRE DAME, INDIANA
DESIGNED BY FRANK O. WILLIAMS
LIBRARY OF CONGRESS CATALOG NUMBER: 66-24924
MANUFACTURED IN THE UNITED STATES OF AMERICA

TO MY FATHER
WHO ENCOMPASSED THE CITY
IN A SINGLE VIEW

# CREDITS

t—top; b—bottom

ii   Litton Industries,
     Aero Service
     Division
2    Litton Industries,
     Aero Service
     Division
5    Litton Industries
     Aero Service
     Division
9    Litton Industries,
     Aero Service
     Division
13   Ewing Galloway
15   The Port of New
     York Authority
16   Bob Sterling Photo
24   Carnegie Institution
     of Washington
25   Carnegie Institution
     of Washington
26   U.S. Bureau of the
     Census
30   Stokes Collection,
     New York
     Public Library
31   Library of Congress
32   Library of Congress
34t  U.S. Bureau of
     Public Roads
35   U.S. Bureau of
     Public Roads
36t  U.S. Coast and
     Geodetic Survey
36b  Pennsylvania
     Avenue
     Commission,
     Edmund Barrett
37   The Smithsonian
     Institution

39   U.S. Bureau of the
     Census
40   The Smithsonian
     Institution
41   Carnegie Institution
     of Washington
43   The Smithsonian
     Institution
45   Wide World Photos
46   The Smithsonian
     Institution
47   Culver Pictures,
     Inc.
49   The Smithsonian
     Institution
53   The Smithsonian
     Institution
54   The Bettman
     Archive
56   Ewing Galloway
57   U.S. Bureau of
     Public Roads
58   U.S. Bureau of
     Public Roads
59   Ewing Galloway
63   Ewing Galloway
66   Perkins and Will
     Partnership;
     Louis Checkman
     Photo
69   City of New York,
     Housing and
     Redevelopment
     Board
70t  Redevelopment
     Authority of
     the City of
     Philadelphia;
     Lawrence S.
     Williams Photo

70b  Redevelopment
     Authority of
     the City of
     Philadelphia;
     Shecktor Photo
72t  Redevelopment
     Authority of
     the City of
     Philadelphia;
     Lawrence S.
     Williams Photo
72b  Redevelopment
     Authority of
     the City of
     Philadelphia;
     Shecktor Photo
77   City of Hartford
     Redevelopment
     Agency
78   Redevelopment
     Authority of
     the City of
     Philadelphia;
     Lawrence S.
     Williams Photo
79   Redevelopment
     Authority of
     the City of
     Philadelphia;
     Lawrence S.
     Williams Photo
80   Keyes, Lethbridge,
     and Condon;
     J. Alexander
     Photo
81   Keyes, Lethbridge,
     and Condon;
     J. Alexander
     Photo

82t Redevelopment
  Authority of
  the City of
  Philadelphia;
  Shecktor Photo
82b Redevelopment
  Authority of
  the City of
  Philadelphia;
  Gilbert and Ring
  Photo
85 New Haven
  Redevelopment
  Agency; Noel
  Fehm Photo
86 U.S. Urban
  Renewal
  Administration
87 U.S. Urban
  Renewal
  Administration
95 National Trust
  for Historic
  Preservation;
  Norman Matheny
96 Perkins & Will
  Partnership
99 National Trust
  for Historic
  Preservation
103 New Haven
  Redevelopment
  Agency; Noel
  Fehm Photo
109 U.S. Bureau of
  Public Roads
110 U.S. General
  Services
  Administration
111 U.S. General
  Services
  Administration;
  Louis Checkman

112–113 U.S. General
  Services
  Administration;
  Louis Checkman
114 Leonard R.
  Greenup,
  National Trust
  for Historic
  Preservation
115 Leonard R.
  Greenup,
  National Trust
  for Historic
  Preservation
116 National Trust
  for Historic
  Preservation
117 Charles Luckman
  Associates;
  National Trust
  for Historic
  Preservation
119 National Trust
  for Historic
  Preservation;
  Lawrence S.
  Williams Photo
123 Adapted from
  U.S. Bureau
  of Census Data
126 U.S. Bureau of
  Public Roads
127 The Washington
  Post
129 Wide World Photos
131 Mills, Petticord,
  and Mills;
  Davis Studio
132t Author's collection
133 Downtown
  Progress, Inc.,
  Washington,
  D.C.;
  Architect: Keyes,
  Lethbridge,
  and Condon

134 National Capital
  Transportation
  Agency
136 Ewing Galloway
139 Author's collection
141 Wide World Photos
144 U.S. Bureau of
  Public Roads
145 U.S. Bureau of
  Public Roads
148 Author's collection
149 Carnegie
  Institution
  of Washington
150 Author's collection
151 U.S. Bureau of
  Public Roads
153t U.S. Bureau of
  Public Roads
153b Author's collection
154t U.S. Bureau of
  Public Roads
154b Author's collection
156 Author's collection
158 Author's collection
159 Author's collection
160 Author's collection
161 New York
  Central System;
  National Trust
  for Historic
  Preservation
162 Author's collection
164 Author's collection
165 Author's collection
167 Author's collection
168 Author's collection
169 Author's collection
171 Downtown
  Progress, Inc.,
  Washington,
  D.C.
173 Author's collection
174 Author's collection
175 Author's collection

176 U.S. General
      Services
      Administration
177 U.S. General
      Services
      Administration
178 Author's collection
179 Author's collection
181 Author's collection
183 *The Washington
      Post*
184 Author's collection
185 Author's collection
186 Author's collection
187 Author's collection
188 Author's collection
189 Author's collection
190 Author's collection
191 Author's collection
193 *The Washington
      Post;* Frank Hoy
      Photo
194 Author's collection
196t The Budd Company
196b St. Louis Car
      Company,
      Division of
      General Steel
      Industries
198 *Scientific American*
199 Tube Transit, Inc.
200 Westinghouse
      Electric
      Corporation
201 Westinghouse
      Electric
      Corporation
202 Philadelphia
      City Planning
      Commission
203 Philadelphia
      City Planning
      Commission
205 U.S. Bureau of
      Public Roads

206 Teletran
      Corporation
207 Louis I. Kahn
208 Columbia
      University
      in the City of
      New York,
      School of
      Architecture
209 Columbia Uni-
      versity in the City
      of New York,
      School of
      Architecture
212 National Capital
      Transportation
      Agency
215 National Capital
      Planning
      Commission
217 National Capital
      Planning
      Commission
219 National Capital
      Planning
      Commission
221 National Capital
      Planning
      Commission
226 Whittlesey
      and Conklin
227 Whittlesey
      and Conklin
228 Whittlesey
      and Conklin
229 Whittlesey
      and Conklin
230 Whittlesey
      and Conklin
231 Author's collection
232 Author's collection
233 Author's collection
235 Community Re-
      search and De-
      velopment, Inc.

236 Community Re-
      search and De-
      velopment, Inc.
237 Community
      Research and
      Development,
      Inc.
238 Community
      Research and
      Development,
      Inc.; Ezra Stoller
239 Community
      Research and
      Development,
      Inc.; Ezra Stoller
      Photo
243 Bancroft
      Construction
      Corporation;
      Louis Checkman
      Photo
244 New Haven
      Redevelopment
      Agency;
      Ezra Stoller
      Photo
245 New Haven
      Redevelopment
      Agency;
      Hedrich Blessing
      Photo
247 Author's collection
248 John F. Kennedy
      Center
250 Mills, Petticord,
      and Mills
252 Pennsylvania
      Avenue
      Commission
253 Pennsylvania
      Avenue
      Commission

# PREFACE

THE SHAPING of a significant and orderly urban environment will pose the greatest challenge to our civilization for the rest of this century. In the United States this challenge is most clearly visible in the oldest urbanized region, the Northeast seaboard. The urban spaces of this area testify to both the accomplishments and the failures of man to remain the master of his environment. With urbanization the cities and spaces of this region, self-contained in the past, converged together and became contiguous. The city center lost its simplicity, and spatial relationships became much more closely interwoven. The cities themselves lost much of their identity, and many of their problems became insoluble within their own confines.

Today almost all of the cities of this region are being redeveloped, but with two major shortcomings: they are still being approached as individual entities rather than as parts of a regional whole, and they are being developed without a full appreciation of the importance of cultural continuity. In this whole process the arts and humanities are being badly neglected.

The imaginative shaping of our urban environment is capable of producing great evolutionary feats; it is also capable of continuing and enhancing the great cultural traditions of the eighteenth and nineteenth centuries. Since we shall not have another such opportunity as we do today to rebuild our cities, this book has been written in the hope that it will stimulate a new look at the problems that confront us and generate some new thoughts about the methods for solving them.

The author's interest in the process of shaping central urban spaces of this region was first stimulated fifteen years ago by the faculties of planning, architecture, and the history of art at Yale University. Although the author owes a debt of gratitude to many members of these faculties for their stimulating guidance, there are three whose vision and synoptic view of the art of city design have had the most vital effect upon shaping the subject of this book: Christopher Tunnard, responsible for initiating the pioneering study of the regional growth and esthetics of the megalopolis; Louis Kahn, deeply committed to creating significant urban spaces and forms; and Vincent Scully, Jr., who brought out the full poetic potentialities of the nineteenth century spatial experimentation which forms the roots of our present cultural development.

During the early stages of the preparation of this manuscript various faculty members of the University of Notre Dame and the George Washington University contributed their opinions and suggestions. Also gratefully acknowledged is the cooperation of the many professional organizations and municipal and federal agencies. Particularly useful assistance was obtained from the following: the Urban Renewal Administration of the Department of Housing and Urban Development; the Bureau of Public Roads and the Census Bureau of the Department of Commerce; the Library of Congress; the Smithsonian Institution; the National Trust for Historic Preservation; the John F. Kennedy Center for the Performing Arts; the Carnegie Institution of Washington; and the New York Public Library. Also the Planning Commissions and Redevelopment Agencies of the cities of Boston, Providence, New Haven, Hartford, New York, Philadelphia, Baltimore, and Washington; designers of the new towns of Reston and Columbia and of individual urban projects; Downtown Progress of Washington, D.C. and the National Capital Transportation Agency. And, finally, the American Institute of Planners and the American Institute of Architects.

As this book goes to press, the newly created Department of Housing and Urban Development is undergoing a major reorganization that will involve changes in a majority of the federal urban programs under its jurisdiction.

The author's thanks go also to all who assisted personally in this work, particularly to my wife for her patience and understanding, and to Miss Emily Schossberger, Director of the University of Notre Dame Press for personal interest and guidance in presenting this work.

J. E. K.

*Washington, D.C.*
*January* 1966

# CONTENTS

I. THE SYNOPTIC DESIGN: IN SEARCH OF A MEANING, 3

    1. *Goals and Objectives,* 3
    2. *The Animated Center,* 7
    3. *A Single View,* 22

II. THE VIRILE ROOTS: THE EVOLUTION OF URBANIZATION IN AMERICA, 29

    1. *The Genesis of Urban Growth,* 29
    2. *The Robust Cities,* 38
    3. *The Era of Epic Movement,* 52

III. CREATIVE FEDERALISM: FROM SLUM CLEARANCE TO URBAN DEVELOPMENT, 64

    1. *Emerging Action,* 64
    2. *Redevelopment and Renewal,* 68
    3. *A New Charter,* 84

IV. THE CONVERGING STREAMS: THE NEED FOR BALANCE AND UNITY, 90

    1. *The Invisible Design and the Visible Plan,* 90
    2. *Controls for Macrourbanism,* 97
    3. *The New Urban Entrepreneurs,* 104

V. THE DOLEFUL CITY: THE DILEMMA OF CHANGING PATTERNS, 122

    1. *Urban Quicksilver,* 122
    2. *The Cast-Outs,* 135
    3. *Hub Dynamics,* 142

VI. THE METROPOLIS OF AMERICA: GREAT EXPECTATIONS, 147

    1. *Terminal Temples,* 147
    2. *The Operative Urban Places,* 166
    3. *Slums and Monuments,* 182

VII. URBAN REAPPRAISAL: SHAPING THE EMERGING CONURBATION, 195

    1. *The Megalopolitan Traveler,* 195
    2. *The Search for Form-Coherence,* 214
    3. *Past is Prologue,* 223

VIII. THE CULTURAL RENAISSANCE: NEW FORMS AND SPACES, 225

    1. *The New Satellites,* 225
    2. *Imageability and Imagination,* 240
    3. *The Form-Givers,* 242

IX. CONSPECTUS: TOWARD THE FULFILLMENT OF PROMISE, 257

    1. *The New Hierarchy,* 257
    2. *Policy Planning,* 261
    3. *Cultural Continuity,* 265

BIBLIOGRAPHY, 269

INDEX, 277

# INTRODUCTION

THE LAST TWO DECADES have witnessed a flood of books attempting to portray our urban revolution—books on urban sociology, history, geography, architecture, political science, and related topics. At the same time there has been a dire poverty of critical analyses that tackle in a broad cultural context and comprehensive manner the dynamics of urban design —the movement towards a truly "synoptic" approach to shaping our large urbanized regions and the design of cities. Missing have been critical studies of the processes shaping the environment of America's land of urban promise—the Northeast urbanized region of the United States —and solutions guiding its development through realistic and highly imaginative design. Answering this need constitutes the significant contribution of Professor Julian Kulski's analysis and suggestions.

The importance of urban design as a force in the orderly development of the megalopolis is by and large little understood and appreciated. This condition is mainly due to the lack of an intimate cross-fertilization of ideas among those in sociology, economics, political science, and urban design working toward a synoptic approach. This has occurred partly because of the unwillingness on the part of socioeconomic planners to embrace the new ideology of their counterparts in the area of design and also because of the still-existing wide gulf between the scholar-researchers and those actively engaged in the redevelopment of our urban areas. The need for a greater participation in policy planning and decision-making at all governmental levels on the part of America's leading urban designers was forcefully brought forth by President John F. Kennedy. His call for a unified interdisciplinary attack on the problems of the American city and for a greater emphasis on creative design, cultural continuity, and a new and vigorous national urban philosophy has gone largely unheeded. The urban problems are still being approached through a timid, largely unimaginative, and compartmentalized manner. The use of America's design talent remains largely untapped, and the training of future "synoptic designers" has still not been faced by our government and universities.

The last chapter of this book includes some pointed suggestions of how to repair the damage done to our cities by shortsighted planning methods, undistinguished architecture, and the lack of a positive design philosophy. These contributions, which call for immediate educational and legislative implementation, are interesting and carefully documented throughout the book. Dr. Kulski's selection of examples makes clear the need for urban design at all levels of the urban development process and indicates that we have already begun, although in a hesitant way, to express the shaping of virile, fresh, urban forms through creative synoptic design—a process that has roots deep in our history and opens up exciting new avenues for future urban environment.

The reader will find pages on the historical evolution of the Northeast conurbation of particular interest in that they contain a new and positive interpretation of nineteenth-century urban development, outline the vital role of changing modes of travel upon the emerging form of American urban development, and afford a deeper understanding of the gradual functional and artistic changes that took place during the last two centuries.

The critical analysis of the Urban Renewal Program from its inception to the first days of the Department of Housing and Urban Development deserves a careful scrutiny. Despite their superficial success, the achievements of communities that have used this tool in their attempt to bring about a cultural, social, and aesthetic renaissance point to a much more meaningful, socially more valuable, and culturally more significant use of urban development. In spite of the author's intentional desire to portray the positive results of urban renewal and the efforts of a handful of capable professional planners and designers to create fully integrated, exciting urban spaces, the reader will find his analysis pointing to a whole gamut of unsatisfactory solutions and unfulfilled challenges and promises: the skirting of the need for efficient mass transportation, inter- and intra-city, by supporting largely obsolescent and expensive private motor vehicles as the basis of urban development; inadequate participation and understanding of creative urban development on the part of the law-makers; and the lack of a visible imprint of the designer's skills upon our renewed areas. Equally emphasized is the largely ineffective machinery that exists in our large metropolitan areas for planning and controlling the development of the social, physical, and cultural activities forming its very essence. Through the universality of his presentation the author has enabled the student of urban affairs to draw his own conclusions, to separate the pedestrian and the mundane from the brilliant and the so-phisticated, and to stimulate the young into this exciting and challenging field of human endeavor.

The author's response to the challenge of designing meaningful and significant urban spaces is best described in his own words and does not require further elaboration on my part. Professor Kulski's training in the art of city planning began very early and dates to his observations of the accomplishments of his father, then the vice president of the City of Warsaw, in the prewar renewal of this old and historic European capital. The author completed his design and planning studies at the School of Art and Architecture at Yale University, soon after to immerse himself completely in the professional practice of city design. In the early years of the Urban Planning Assistance Program and urban renewal experi-mentations the author pioneered in diverting the emphasis of communities for which he planned from a two-dimensional, statistically oriented ap-proach to the comprehensive urban design conspectus of action-oriented programs. His interest in the design of urban open spaces and total archi-tecture dates to those early years, and it was this dedication to design that led him eventually to combine his professional work with teaching. During these active years as a designer and scholar he strove continuously to bring together administrators and creative urban designers, often representing diametrically opposed interests, philosophies, and approaches. It is in this area of influencing reconciliation and common understanding among the social and administrative planners and the forces of creative design that is constituted one of Dr. Kulski's major achievements. In sharing his experiences and thoughts with students concerned with urban design the future leaders of urban America can benefit not only by his experience but above all by his dedication to the cause of mastering our urban environment and of creating urban spaces in the best American tradition, embodying the highest aesthetic, social, and cultural ideals.

DANIEL URBAN KILEY

*Wings Point, Charlotte, Vermont*
*Summer,* 1966

LAND OF URBAN PROMISE

*New York City.*

## I. THE SYNOPTIC DESIGN: IN SEARCH OF A MEANING

### 1. GOALS AND OBJECTIVES

There is almost a blind faith in the forthcoming century as a period of great resurgency of American civilization. This faith is expressed in economic expansion, in building, in the acceptance of responsibilities abroad, in a willingness to do what is necessary, regardless of whether it is popular. This mood contrasts strongly with older civilizations, which are more preoccupied with refinements, and with developing nations, which are too involved with the immediate and pressing needs of building an industrial base to have a very intimate and living faith in the future.

Like other great civilizations of the past, this one will be known for its building activities—frantic construction, constant action as opposed to stalemate, particularly in urban areas. Yet at this moment urban development is not being approached either from a synoptic viewpoint or according to a well-defined plan. The rebuilding of city centers is not being conducted according to a theoretical formula; it is being done by a ruggedly confident faith, a faith that is in the virile tradition of the last 200 years. It is an approach which has great vitality but also one which makes over-all planning intrinsically difficult. Whether the future will justify this faith cannot now be known. Today America is too busy, too involved, to analyze introspectively what it is doing.

In this era of frenzied activity a clear sense of objectives and direction has become blurred, and many basic concepts that existed up to the era of industrialization and urbanization have become emasculated. This situation calls for a deep probing of national purpose and intent. This need is especially apparent in domestic programs concerned with urban problems. Although the analysis of semantics is outside the scope of this discussion, a few general, recurring concepts need to be re-examined and understood in order to overcome existing misconceptions. Among these are "design" and "planning," which need redefinition from their commonly accepted, often ambiguous, sense in a truer and more meaningful sense.

In the past "planning" meant representation of things in physical terms—drawings, maps, sketches, statistics. Today this concept has been broadened to encompass the total gamut of life processes. This usage is chaotic because, on the one hand, it has led to a loss of the original meaning of the word and, on the other hand, it has obscured the specific meaning it has in today's world.

This confusion is further compounded by the meaning of the concept "design." In its broad, original sense design meant purpose and intent. As commonly used and understood today, it has been narrowed to mean the patterning of things—clothes, houses, automobiles, cities. Since design should be defined as purpose and intent, it is misleading to apply it in a purely physical sense.

Design in the true sense is much more concerned with the multifaceted aspects of meaning than simply creating abstract forms in a vacuum. Design is an expression of a way of life; of political, social, and legal institutions; of time in history; and of peoples. Design should not be used in a narrow, constrictive, and dividing sense. It should be used to mean a positive, vital force, truly comprehensive in that it is involved in defining purpose and intent of goals and objectives as well as by giving them forms which truly and honestly express them.

An attempt to apply the concept of design to urban ecology has given birth to the term "urban design." Before this term was even defined, it was pigeonholed to become yet another attempt to extend the narrow meaning of design, but simply on a larger scale. Urban design has thus commonly come to be accepted as purely the physical design

of cities. But this is a gross misconception, since it is not possible to have physical design as distinct from other social components. Design must include all factors that make up the city. In this definition design is truly comprehensive in that it contains a sense of intent and purpose of the total environment.

The rebuilding of central urban spaces of American cities and the formation of new urban centers within the evolving conurbations will constitute one of the chief national concerns for the rest of this century. Therefore, a major effort must be directed toward identifying present trends and conditions caused by the rapid urbanization of the United States and finding ways to achieve more meaningful and significant urban spaces.

The present undertaking touches upon the many and varied aspects of urban life and development. It does not stress any one aspect of the many functions of the urban complex, such as transportation or housing, but attempts to take a synoptic view of the underlying problems; it does not examine theories or philosophies of planning under different types of governmental systems. It is a study of government controls, legal reforms, and design theories involved in rebuilding urban America, and particularly its urban centers. It is a search for ways to make American urban complexes well-functioning, efficient organisms and to allow their component parts to grow and develop in concert with each other as integral elements of a single, enormous urban region.

Although the urbanization of the American continent has affected all urban areas, the Northeast Atlantic region provides a dramatic example of the evolving nature and form of urban cores under the impact of population explosion, changing modes of transportation, automation, and cultural and educational growth. This great geographic area contains a large percentage of the different types of urban spaces found in American urban galaxies, and for this reason it has been selected as the most promising one on which to focus.

## 2. THE ANIMATED CENTER

In the first 50 years of this century, according to the United States Census Bureau, the number of people living in metropolitan areas rose from 24 million to over 84 million. This number is expected to double by 1975, when 66 percent of the United States population will reside in metropolitan areas and the total urban population will amount to over 75 percent of an expected total population of 240 million.

The idea of central urban spaces is increasingly receiving the attention it deserves, but there is a glaring vacuum in theoretical work in this vital field. There is little agreement on what a central urban space is, which is not surprising when considered in the light that the city itself has almost entirely lost its connotation, traditional form, and urban entity under the pressure of urbanization. With the body becoming more and more amorphous it is increasingly harder to locate and define its "centers," while at the same time it becomes increasingly crucial to do so in order to shape and direct the growth of the entire urban structure.

The city's expansion far beyond its political boundaries to encompass large regions has made metropolitan planning the number one planning problem of this century. The metropolitan urban entity as a functional unit is organized around one or more central cities as its focal point of dominance. About these are located subcenters with the institutions and services that cater to this conurbation as a whole. The overlapping of metropolitan areas during the last 20 years within the framework of a much larger geographic unit in some parts of the country has tended to further break up and obscure the identity of the city and added another vital dimension to metropolitan planning problems.

To classify, in a very general way, urban entities purely according to their size and density of development, the smallest urban grouping can be considered a residential subneighborhood of approximately 500 people; at the second level would be the neighborhood with anywhere up to 3,000 people; at the third, either an individual small city or a sector of a large one, amounting to up to 100,000 people; at the fourth, cities up to 1,000,000; at the fifth, the important urban complexes up to 10,000,000; and finally on the ladder of the hierarchy of urban systems is the conurbation, a region containing many cities and a multitude of subcenters, yet organized into an easily distinguishable and cohesive form. These conurbations have central urban spaces arranged into highly individual, dynamic, and organic relationships. These regions, lately referred to as megalopolises, vary widely in the size of their population, densities of their centers, and their function, form, and geophysical characteristics. There are eight such large urbanized complexes around major cities which fall into this classification at the present time in the United States: Los Angeles-San Francisco, Seattle-Portland, Houston-New Orleans, Daytona-Miami, Atlanta-Raleigh, Columbus-Cincinnati-Louisville, Chicago-Detroit-Pittsburgh, and Boston-New York-Washington.

The last of these, the oldest and most populous, has been described by the French geographer, Jean Gottmann, as megalopolis in the following words: "The main axis of the region is about 600 miles long and the width varies between 30 and 100 miles. The total area amounts to 53,575 square miles, or 1.8 percent of the land of the 48-state United States. . . . The population of Megalopolis was close to 31.9 million in 1950, or 21 percent of the total population of the continental United States. It was about 37 million in 1960."[1]

To make the investigation of trends and formulation of conclusions of the megalopolitan central urban spaces more meaningful, the following general classification of urban centers may be useful for discussion purposes: *attraction potential,* based upon geographic sphere of influence—world, continental, megalopolitan, city, town, neighborhood;

[1] Jean Gottman, *Megalopolis* (New York: The Twentieth Century Fund, 1961), p. 26.

*functional primacy,* depending on predominant use, function, and purpose—governmental, commercial, industrial, transportation, recreational, residential; *spatial form,* according to principal physical characteristics—dense unregulated vertical, planned vertical, dense unplanned horizontal, balanced, predominantly open, inorganic non-nuclear, animated nuclear.

## Attraction Potential

In an urbanizing world certain urban centers tend to exert a worldwide scale of influence and to become a pole of attraction, and this trend will gain momentum with increased global transportation and communication in the future. Examples of world urban centers are the cores of greater London, Paris, New York, Tokyo, and other capitals of the world whose urban magnetic "attractiveness" knows no national boundaries.[2]

In the second line of this mainly geographic hierarchy are continental urban centers that generate intellectual, cultural, and political life over many countries and that can be considered the centers of urban civilization of certain sections of the world. Rome in Western Europe, Warsaw in Eastern Europe, and Rio de Janeiro in South America are illustrations of important metropolitan international centers.

With the creation in many parts of the world of regional "giant cities," the megalopolitan urban centers are a relatively new phenomenon. In the United States the Northeast Megalopolis contains a great range and variety of interdependent and interconnected urban cores. The major hard cores of this particular megalopolitan example are the

[2] One of the most outspoken writers on the problems of world and continental urban centers is Lewis Mumford who in 1932 criticized the then proposed New York regional plan for not recognizing the real problems of the metropolis as those basically of "continental and world-wide conditions." "The Plan of New York," *New Republic,* June 15, 1932, and June 22, 1932.

centers of Boston, Providence, Hartford, New Haven, New York, Newark, Philadelphia, Baltimore, and Washington. The characteristics, trends, patterns, and areas of influence of these urban centers have altered traditional concepts.

The city centers have undergone radical changes in nature, function, and form under many influences, among which amalgamation, concentration, and decentralization are illustrative. Reflecting the changing nature of the city, they have lost their traditional role and have acquired new concepts and new responsibilities. The integration of old towns and the development of new satellite towns within the metropolitan and megalopolitan urban structure have also greatly affected the character of the town centers by placing them into a complex net of functions and services, thus destroying their primary characteristics of self-sufficiency and a certain degree of independence.

As the urban colossus grows in area and mass, the need for human scale becomes ever more important, as does the need for neighborhood urban centers as an element of urban scale easily comprehensible and related to the individual. This one issue of planning has been recognized and studied mostly at the expense of the much more complex problem of the comprehensive, balanced relationship of all urban centers within a region in communion with each other.

*Functional Primacy*

A classification of urban centers according to their primary use and function can be arrived at in only a general way since functional activities are continually changing and becoming increasingly amalgamated against the background of new urban conditions. The present trend of ever-increasing centralization and growth of the national government, brought about by the process of urbanization, has not only changed the federal-state-county-municipal government relationships but has also brought new requirements for every level of government and with it new functions and expressions of government urban centers. Centralization of government activities is greatly affecting the planning and shaping of urban centers in the capitals; similarly the increased responsibility and activity of municipal and urban county governments in local affairs is altering the character of the old "civic center." The government center in its urban connotation in America today is no longer a "town square" surrounded by public buildings; rather it is a more sophisticated concept of large central sectors of urban space forming the core of all types of government activity.

Among the urban centers that have been greatly affected by urban sprawl and urban population explosion, the old "central business districts" have been significantly hurt, economically and physically, by the trek to the suburbs and the postwar development of "shopping centers." The resultant loss of the power to attract and influence on the part of the center-city, and the flight of revenue to suburban centers, have turned most American "hearts of the city" into slums and blight. This cancer was the first indication of the growing sickness of the city and a sign that a new concept of commercial centers was required. An analysis of retail sales over a six-year period, as reported in 1962, showed that in the retail sections of 45 metropolitan areas, retail sales rose 32 percent—but only 1.6 percent in central business districts, indicating a dramatic trend of emigration of retail businesses out of the center-city to the suburbs.

The commercial center in the 1960's is an urban commercial space and includes neighborhood shopping areas, fringe shopping areas, satellite shopping areas as well as the older downtown centers, which are undergoing major surgery and rejuvenation. The loss on the part of the city center of the prewar commercial monopoly through decentralization of the commercial empire has had a significant impact upon the shaping of urban cores.

Automation, greater emphasis upon industry-connected research activities, and trends toward decentralization of production have turned many industrial centers into ghost spaces and pockets of unemployment, abandoned buildings, deterioration, and blight. The once-powerful industrial centers of Pennsylvania, New York, and other states of the Northeast Megalopolis have lost their physical centroidal characteristics. Today, in lieu of a few, there are many industrial urban centers: centers of research, centers of parts manufacturing, and centers of assembly.

The greatest change that the postwar era has brought upon urban spaces has been in the area of transportation. The freeways and the airlines, having superseded the railways as the important carriers of passengers in the field of intercity transportation, have made many an important urban railroad junction obsolete almost overnight. As the result of this great decrease in railroad activities, almost all major urban centers in the United States are facing the large task of removing or consolidating obsolete, centrally located railroad lines out of the heart of the city as an integral part of the renewal of their central spaces; Philadelphia was one of the first to accomplish this goal. Providence's plan called for removal of tracks out of an 80-acre area and development on this reclaimed land of a completely new civic center, to include a heliport-garage, passenger station, cultural center, science museum, hotel, city hall, and state and federal office buildings.[3]

The new urban transportation centers became the airport, usually located outside old city limits; the bus terminal, an often huge, traffic-generating facility located throughout the Northeast Megalopolis; the rapid transit station; and finally the parking facility. Instead of a single-function transportation center of the past, the new one is a conglomeration of many modes of transportation. The proposed urban transportation center in the heart of Philadelphia is integrating the railroad and rapid-transit station with intracity and long-distance intercity bus facilities.

[3] Providence City Plan Commission, *Downtown Providence 1970* (Providence, 1961), pp. 128–135.

*New York Port Authority Bus Terminal. A brutal and illogical placement of
a large urban transportation center almost completely unintegrated with other
modes of transportation. Instead of being a true megalopolitan multimode
transportation center, this facility only adds to the already chaotic and confused urban environment.*

THE SYNOPTIC DESIGN    15

*Lincoln Center of the Performing Arts, New York City.*

This mammoth transportation center is integrated with smaller satellite transportation centers on the outskirts of urban fringe areas providing parking for the "park and ride" system. The multimode transportation center will in the future form the center of development of all megalopolitan hubs.

While urban commercial and industrial centers in the second half of the twentieth century show tendencies towards deconcentration, cultural life, accelerated by the process of urbanization, tends towards a fuller, more concrete, and more centralized expression. At the present time the construction of and plans for building urban cultural centers is proceeding on an unpredecented scale. The new Lincoln Center of the Performing Arts in New York and the proposed John F. Kennedy Center in Washington are typical of the magnetic cultural concentration in the hubs of the Northeast Megalopolis. The "attraction" sphere of influence of cultural life of the nation's capital is expected to more than double within the next 20 years. By 1980, 35 million people a year are expected to visit Washington, compared with 15.4 million in 1960. This influx of tourists to the nation's central urban space will raise Washington to the forefront of the world's urban visitor centers.[4] These urban centers are not limited to one or a few buildings arranged around a central open space but tend to form the very heart of cultural life of the region and to integrate with other activities of central urban life. This trend towards the development of indigenous cultural life along the decentralized and integrated modes of urban living is clearly recognizable in the development of new satellite urban centers. The designers of the most recent megalopolitan new town—Columbia, located between Washington and Baltimore—have indicated their objections to the compartmentalization of cultural activities in large cultural centers. Their outlook on culture as a pervasive, integral, and subtle influence upon the everyday life of

[4] National Capital Downtown Committee, *Action Plan for Downtown* (Downtown Progress Inc., 1962), p. 12.

urban dwellers is exemplified by the wide range of cultural functions consciously integrated with other central functions of their planned community: a large theatre, a concert hall, library, dance center, family life institute, art school, and craft center.

Among the important elements which are being amalgamated are the previously distinct and separate park and recreation spaces. The prewar urban recreation centers, the parks and playgrounds, are being more and more integrated into the over-all structure of central urban spaces, in line with the philosophy that recreation should not be separated from everyday urban life of the center city. The open spaces of the "downtown"—the streets, squares, and malls—are beginning to be recognized as spaces that should be fully utilized for human recreation and enjoyment.

The residential center in the urban core is often more invisible than visible and is comprised of a complexity of subtle expressions of interior and exterior spaces—spontaneous rather than organized in character. In her attack upon traditional orthodox urban planning methods of zoning central urban spaces according to simple primary uses, Jane Jacobs suggests that the urban residential districts should have a mixture of primary uses to guarantee the diversity and vitality of truly urban life. She says: "When a city heart stagnates or disintegrates, a city as a social neighborhood of the whole begins to suffer: people who ought to get together, by means of central activities that are failing, fail to get together. Ideas and money that ought to meet, and do so often by happenstance in a place of central vitality, fail to meet. The networks of city public life develop gaps they cannot afford. Without a strong and inclusive central heart, a city tends to become a collection of interests isolated from one another. It falters at producing something greater, socially, culturally, and economically, than the sum of its separate parts."[5]

[5] Jane Jacobs, *The Death and Life of Great American Cities* (New York: Random House, 1961), p. 165.

*Spatial Form*

The last of the three aforementioned categories, in dealing with the form and space of the urban core, can be classified in only a rather general and theoretical way, as every central urban space, being man-conceived and man-created, must be highly individual. Nevertheless, it is possible to discuss certain common spatial characteristics of the urban core.

The Northeast Megalopolis contains a few good examples of the dense, unregulated, vertical urban center. These centers are unregulated by a central compositional thought or by urban design considerations and design controls; they are regulated simply by geographic and economic conditions and forces and to a lesser degree by a two-dimensional grid system. This type of center dominates the rest of the city by virtue of its size, intensity, and visual impact. Mid-Manhattan provides the most striking case of these skyscraping enclosed forms. They also appear on a smaller scale in the centrums of Boston and Philadelphia. This general spatial form is distinguished by the following characteristics: predominance of the bulk and mass of buildings, microstonescape in lieu of landscape, extremes of scale, great variety, and simplification of the image by omission.

In contrast to the densely built-up, densely populated, unregulated and largely unplanned centers of old New York, Boston, and Philadelphia is a rather new concept of the planned vertical urban center that in recent years has appeared as the result of postwar redevelopment activities. Charles Center in Baltimore and the new center of Hartford are examples of contemporary attempts at shaping balanced, vertical urban-center forms. These centers are an attempt to bring some qualities into the central urbanscape that have been missing in the older centers—order, space, light, and recognition of the need for separateness between pedestrian spaces and vehicular areas—while at the same time straining to utilize thoroughly the extremely expensive central land through the application of maximum floor-area ratio. These attempts have, however, had only a very limited success in achieving these objectives. The lack of a comprehensive development policy and the general failure to recognize the cultural and historical base of the city have in most cases produced a rather antiseptic and meaningless new urban environment.

As equally little controlled as the unregulated vertical urban centers are the dense, unplanned horizontal urban centers, which for the purposes of this classification are limited to centers with buildings with a maximum height of approximately ten stories. These central urban forms are more common than the vertical prototype. Although they provide a greater degree of light, air, and smaller scale, these older centers share with the vertical urban centers the problems of chaos, tremendous traffic congestion, air pollution, and absence of urban design. Typical of this category are the old downtown sections of cities like Newark, Providence, and Washington. Actually, the absence of urban design is more glaring in the unplanned horizontal urban center than in the vertical, as the lack of unifying building height, lack of unity in building materials, in spatial organization, and in general composition are well within the angle of vision and thus are more obvious and disturbing to sensory perception.

As the result of experimentation with the redevelopment of central urban spaces, there has evolved during the last few years a more vital and a more positive acceptance of social goals in urban development and a greater understanding of the need for a guiding, over-all compositional thought. These directions are expressed in the forms of certain new, balanced, integrated central urban spaces which attempt to mix high buildings with low-rise structures to provide a variety of forms and of spatial experiences within these new centers. The Southwest redevelopment area of the nation's capital is an attempt at conscious juxtaposition of buildings of various heights and shapes to create an organic central composition. These examples must be viewed as rather primitive attempts at giving form and substance to the extremely complex, changing nature of urban life. A much more indigenous, imaginative, and meaningful solution must be arrived at before social, integrative forces can be shaped into an expressive, total, and many-dimensional environment. Such more dynamic solutions would point towards a better understanding of the inherent vital forces and needs of central urban life.

The predominantly open central urban spaces, which recognize that not only stonescape but landscape, not only buildings but also positive spaces, should form an integral part of the center city, are those most rarely found. Washington, as a federal city and the nation's capital, is an exception. Since some of the land in the core of this city belongs to the government, thus having been saved from land speculation, and because the city's original plan foresaw the need for predominantly open spaces in the centrum, Washington's urban fabric is indeed unique.

Two other classifications of the spatial forms of urban centers that are beginning to be clearly distinguished in the present evolution of megalopolitanization should be mentioned. They are the "inorganic non-nuclear urban center" and the "animated nuclear center." The first, regardless of size, is developing without planning and negates the very structure of organized urban life—"an expression of accident, violence, and instability."[6] Humphrey Carver, in describing the loss of form of central urban spaces, blames the "antinucleation" arguments supporting the view that ubiquitous mobility and telecommunication have now released us from any conventional forms of city organization. "The city is an abstract continuum like an infinite, nonobjective painting without recognizable shape or focus; or it might be thought of as plasma in which individuals and families float in a kind of unattached suspense." The animated nuclear center, by contrast, is a well-integrated, functional

[6] Humphrey Carver, *Cities in the Suburbs* (Toronto: University of Toronto Press, 1962), p. 68.

entity truly expressive of cultural and functional interdependence and complexity. The animated nuclear spaces are most expressive of the dynamics of the megalopolis.


3. A SINGLE VIEW

The existing conditions of central urban spaces and the factors which limit urban design today have evolved over a number of years. Since the present form of urban centers was shaped to a large degree by economic and accidental forces and very little by conscious planning, these processes stand in need of re-examination.

For example, the understanding of the effects of changing modes of transportation—water transport, horse-drawn cars, railroads, electrically powered streetcars, and finally the motor car—upon the structure, pattern, function, and form of cities is necessary in order to obtain a synoptic perspective of the problems of central urban spaces. Only from such a vantage point can we approach the design of urban centers. Also, the tradition of individual house ownership and the morphological cycle of the nation's social consciousness (as evidenced by interest in central urban spaces during certain evolutionary periods of the history of urbanization) are some of the illustrative aspects of this great cultural development.

The evolution of the dynamics of urbanization and the development of urban centers from the historical point of view can be viewed against the background of the following basic assumptions:

(1) The nucleus of central urban spaces is people, (2) inadequate transportation means an inadequate central urban space, (3) social conditions make urban design, urban design makes social conditions, and (4) responsibility of government magnifies with the rate of urbanization.

The evolution of central urban spaces in America in the past 200 years can be examined in the light of the above principles. In order to obtain a clearer view of the basic evolutionary factors—population, transportation, social conditions, and the role of government—and their effect upon shaping urban cores, this historical perspective is limited to evolutionary highlights. The first 100 years are interpreted as leading to the outbreak of rural-urban animosities, and the last century of ever-increasing frantic urbanization is seen as eventually evolving a new urban structure—the megalopolis.

In a period of two centuries the population growth in this country increased from approximately 3 million in 1760 to 180 million in 1960, a 60-fold increase. Over the same span of years, the urban population rose more than 600 times, from approximately 210,000 in 1760 to 126 million in 1960, indicating a rate of urbanization ten times the rate of population growth.

Behind these figures lie the problems, factors, and forces of the changing role and form of central urban spaces. Basically, these problems are embedded in the laws of the land, which were originally written for entirely rural conditions, a rural society, and a rural country and not for the development of urban civilization, cities, and central urban spaces. This elemental conflict, built into the laws of the land 200 years ago, has never been successfully resolved and forms one of the basic problems of urban development. The reasons for lack of adequate urban legislation in individual states can be traced to the underrepresentation of the cities in state legislatures caused by a system of political apportionment favoring the rural areas over the urban centers. As late as 1938 not one of the 21 states where the majority of the population was already urban had granted a proportionate share of representation in the state legislature.[7]

[7] Albert Lepawski, "Development of Urban Government," Part I, Vol. I, Supplementary Report of Urbanism Committee to the National Resources Committee (U.S. Government Printing Office: Washington, D.C., 1938).

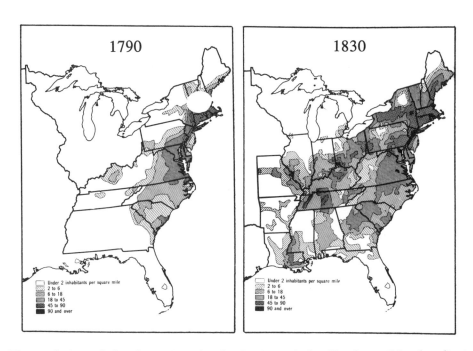

*The evolution of the dynamics of urbanization of the Northeast Megalopolis is dramatically portrayed by the rapid increase in the density of population. By the end of the eighteenth century the present form of this conurbation was already quite well defined, and by the first part of this century all of the major urbanized regions were well formulated and established.*

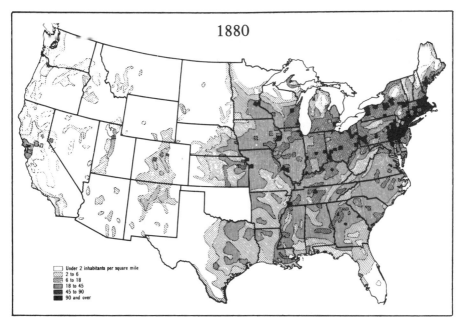

1880

Under 2 inhabitants per square mile
2 to 6
6 to 18
18 to 45
45 to 90
90 and over

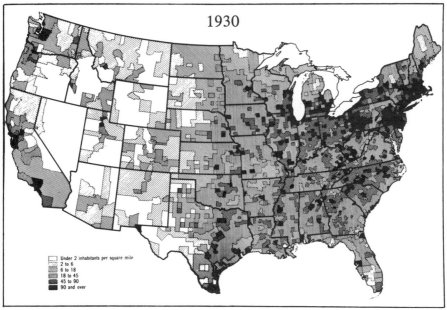

1930

Under 2 inhabitants per square mile
2 to 6
6 to 18
18 to 45
45 to 90
90 and over

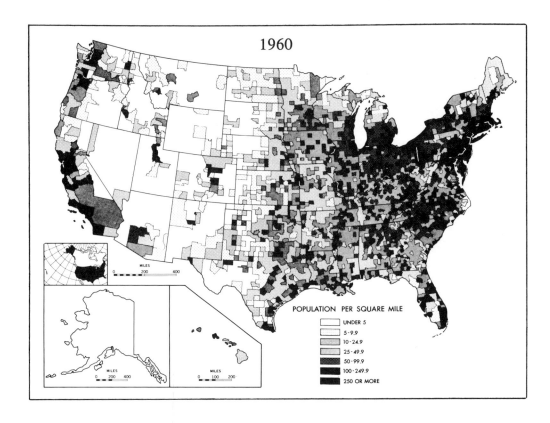

1960

POPULATION PER SQUARE MILE

UNDER 5
5 - 9.9
10 - 24.9
25 - 49.9
50 - 99.9
100 - 249.9
250 OR MORE

To comprehend fully the complexity and ramifications of the urbanization of America, the degree of autonomy of the states must be kept foremost in mind. For example, the states have the right to decide whether they will pass legislation enabling their communities to plan. Since each state's political and socioeconomic climate differs, the enactment of enabling planning legislation did not take place simultaneously and kept cities and towns in some states from planning their central urban spaces until 1961–1962. Today all of the 50 states have enabling legislation for urban planning, and all but two (Louisiana and South Carolina) have active urban renewal legislation.

In recent years this autonomy has been significantly curtailed by an ever-increasing role of the national government in shaping central urban spaces. In enacting the Housing Act of 1949, the Congress acknowledged the fact that clearing the slums and the effectuation of development plans for urban centers was beyond the feasibilities of individual cities. In providing for sharing the cost of reshaping American communities, the Congress admitted the fact that rising municipal expenditures and limited tax resources made the renewal process outside the reach of municipal finances alone and that since the human and economic cost of slums spread beyond the city center, the problem was a national one.

Although the process of urbanization has resulted in a dramatic quantitative explosion, the methods of coping with the resultant problems and the theoretical work necessary for shaping central urban spaces have only lately entered the pioneering stage of development. The balanced urban-design plan—which should combine all individual, social, and economic requirements into a well-orchestrated, well-integrated organizational and three-dimensional entity—has not as yet been applied as a tool for controlled and comprehensive urban development. Only such a synoptic concept will meet the pressing needs and dynamic conditions of urban problems and be an appropriate and capable tool for accomplishing great evolutionary feats.

Unfortunately, the often subtle but vital interrelationship of the visible central urban spaces and the invisible centers of urban life often exerts a divisive influence on those most intimately concerned and engaged in urban development. This influence seriously impairs the efforts aimed at significant development of central urban spaces. Since the form of the urban center is the result of its inner life, and the life within it is in a very real sense shaped by its physical form, the "visible" and "invisible" component factors should be integrally interwoven.

The present lack of adequate methodology and sufficient research in the field of urban and regional planning hampers improvement of design and limits the charting of the future form of urban galaxies. This lack is traced to the fact that urban planning is a relatively new profession and that until quite recently any type of planning was viewed with suspicion. Only recently, with the recognition that this country has become predominantly urban in outlook, has the demand for funds and resources required to carry out large-scale educational and research activities been generated.

The methods used to date for judging the effectiveness of renewing central urban spaces are liable to serious questioning. The local planning authorities who are responsible for the development of renewal plans have inadequate funds for research and thus use unscientific methods for judging the effectiveness of their work. The federal government up to now has employed mainly statistical methods to analyze data on urban renewal on a national scale. Basically, such methods are inadequate as they cannot evaluate the effects of urban renewal in terms of significant urban design or measure the extent of its contribution to the development of the total urban entity.

The present methods must be broadened to include the examination of the ultimate potential effect of renewal upon the future of the American urban structure. The development of research aimed in this direction should be encouraged. Even if at first these theoretical findings are not completely conclusive, they will nevertheless prove useful in practical application to specific projects in pointing out the weakness of presently used methods. Constant and thorough analysis of the effects of shaping and reshaping urban centers would assist metropolitan areas and urbanized regions in approaching urban development with well-defined goals and objectives. In order to be able to formulate these design policies, a truly synoptic Aristotelian perspective of the development of central urban spaces is necessary: "The entire city encompassed in a single view."

## II. THE VIRILE ROOTS: THE EVOLUTION
## OF URBANIZATION IN AMERICA

### 1. THE GENESIS OF URBAN GROWTH

The last two centuries have seen the transformation of the United States from a predominantly rural, virgin, and undeveloped land to the complex urban colossus of today. This transformation is really the history of the shaping of central urban spaces.

The 200 years of urbanization begin in the colonial, rural America of the thirteen original colonies, a region in which today the Northeast Megalopolis is located. In 1765 the urban population of colonial America amounted to less than one-twentieth of the entire colonial population. The first United States population census, taken in 1790, showed that following independence, the urban population—living in places with 2,500 or more population—amounted to only 5.1 percent of the total. These Americans, mainly of Anglo-Saxon descent, were intent on building a new urban environment.

The plans of the early urban centers of the Atlantic seaboard—Boston, New York, Philadelphia, Baltimore, and others—clearly reflect the early Americans' own individual expression of urban culture. Since all of these urban centers were located on or near the seacoast, water played a major role in shaping their function and form. Water routes, the sole means of transportation between the urban centers of the Old World and the young settlements of the New, also provided the main intercity transportation. The magnitude of this form of transportation is exemplified by the Boston fleet, which, as early as 1765, consisted of 600 vessels. In that year there also existed an extensive network of roads; Pennsylvania alone had 9,000 wagons. Inland waterways in the form of canals did not come into existence until after the formation of an independent nation.

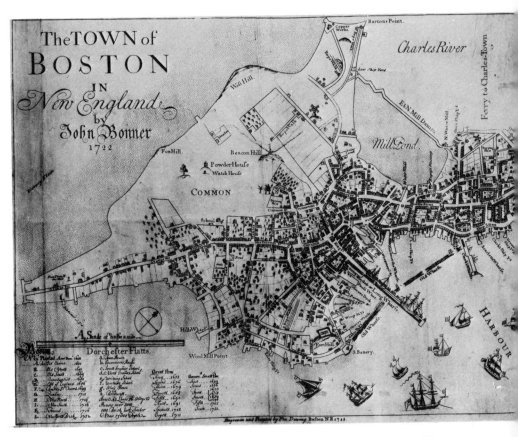

The plan of Boston is an outstanding example of the creation of a significant urban environment out of the wilderness. The full potential of topography is brought forth by exaggerating water and land forms: street patterns follow the natural contours of the land, the fingers of the wharfs accentuate the water forms, landmarks occupy prominent spaces. The entire design expresses the basic purpose and intent of this center—the transportation acropolis of the developing American culture.

*The genius of early American town planners in recognizing strategic locations for the development of centers of urban civilization is expressed in the design for Philadelphia. The choice of the quadripartite scheme, reminiscent of Roman military camps, and the placing of this artifact in the midst of the form defined by the Schuylkill and Delaware rivers, was a virile statement, expressing the inward desire to develop a great, animated democratic culture on this continent.*

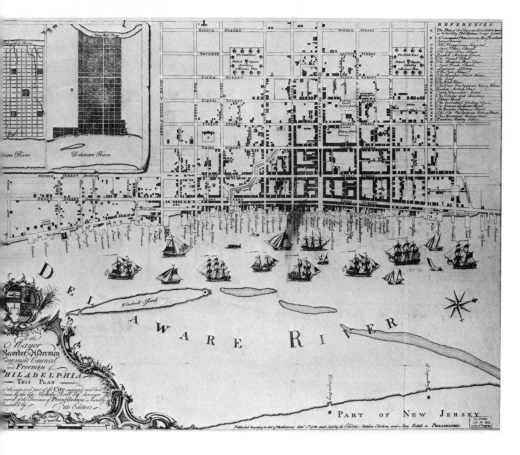

*The selection of the granite plateau island of Manhattan for an urban oasis formed the base of New York's development as the cultural and economic capital of the Americas. Its unique geographic location and topographic features—its many miles of deep, natural harbor; its easily defensible position; and its adaptability to intense urban development—all predetermined its profound future. The inherent suitability of this land for carving complex networks of multilevel underground transportation systems and for creating dense, vertical urban spaces and soaring forms has offered a momentous challenge to man's ability to shape an exciting and meaningful urban environment.*

Although the towns contained a small minority of the total population, the sphere of influence of these early urban centers was enormous in terms of geographic area covered. The five cities which already existed at the time the new republic was formed exerted influences over hundreds of miles. By 1765 these urban centers were truly the centers of culture in America. Harvard University was well established by then, containing a sizable library particularly rich in the field of classical literature. Yale at New Haven, the College of Philadephia (now the University of Pennsylvania), and King's College (now Columbia University) in New York made these urban centers the centers of learning as well.

The role of the government in the first days of the republic was limited chiefly to the development of the laws of the land, protection of urban centers, and construction of a network of roads to unify the widely dispersed and widely different—religiously, ethnographically, and geographically—urban centers of the thirteen states. The framing of the Constitution and its implementation was the chief preoccupation of the first national government. Since the majority of the population of the states was rural, the Constitution was predominantly written for a rural agrarian republic. In 1801, the year that Jefferson, a foe of cities, was inaugurated President, Washington became the capital. Jefferson's wish that America remain a rural country with a rural culture and economy, as well as his dislike of strong, central government, is well known.

The initial period of urbanization that turned the northeastern wilderness into the world's largest megalopolis was marked by a slow but steady flow of people into the urban centers, development of transportation routes, growth of industry, and generally rapid spread of central urban areas. By 1860 eight of the nine cities of America had more than 100,000 population, and of those, five were on the east coast—Philadelphia, Boston, Baltimore, New York, and the latter's suburb, Brooklyn. The 1860 census tabulated almost 400 "urban places" with a

*The Boston Post Road was developed to the point where by 1764 it provided a daily intercity link through a day-and-night post between Boston, Providence, New Haven, and New York. The intercity post-road system had already achieved a distinct regional form cohesion by the end of the eighteenth century.*

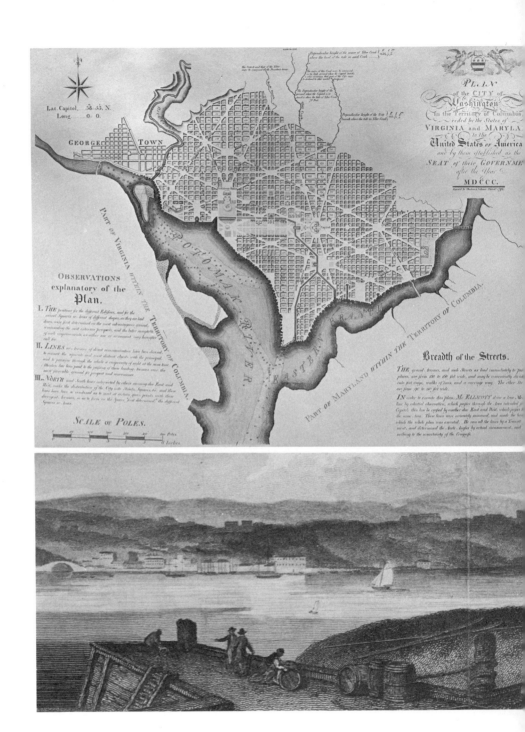

*The selection of the site on the banks of the Potomac River for the Nation's capital was determined in 1790 by Thomas Jefferson and Alexander Hamilton after years of bitter regional rivalries on the part of the states. Following this decision, Major L'Enfant was commissioned by George Washington to design the Federal City, and by 1792 he had developed a plan. In its mature, poetic expression this design represented the highest cultural aspirations of the new republic, and its spatial organization constitutes a masterpiece of the art of urban design.*

*New York City was already a booming metropolis, and the dynamics of its growth required the preparation of an over-all plan for Manhattan. This gigantic design consisted of a gridiron net placed over the entire island, with the central element of the plan a reservoir of open space. This visionary document succeeded in guiding the orderly development of this center for a whole century, during which the population increased almost a hundredfold.*

population over 2,500, with a total urban population of over 6 million—almost 30 times that of 1760 and 4 times that of 1790. Greater New York City in 1860 was a cosmopolis with a population of over 1 million, exceeding all European urban centers of that period except for London and Paris.[1]

## 2. THE ROBUST CITIES

The first 100 years of urbanization and industrialization of the Northeast contributed to the tensions that finally led to the outbreak of the Civil War, which can not only be considered the all-decisive point in the history of the United States but as an epic confrontation of rural-urban animosities. The victory of the more urbanized and industrial North over the predominantly rural South set the beginning of 100 years of ever-increasing frantic urbanization that resulted in the birth of an entirely new historical phenomenon—the megalopolis.

The 50-year period which followed the Civil War was marked by a great increase in the rate of urbanization. The national population doubled during the period between 1860 and 1890, and by 1910 the number of cities with a population over 100,000 had increased from 9 to 50. The census of 1910 lists 228 urban centers with a population of 25,000-plus, with 8 exceeding the half-million mark. In the urban centers of the Northeast the percentages of urban population doubled during this time, while the problems existing in the central urban spaces of those cities became aggravated.

During this period transportation developed at an equally impressive rate. Railroads, which by 1865 became the chief intercity transportation in the east and midwest sections of the United States, began a

[1] U.S. Bureau of the Census, *Current Population Reports, Population Characteristics,* Series P-23, No. 2 (U.S. Government Printing Office: Washington, D.C., 1949), p. 23.

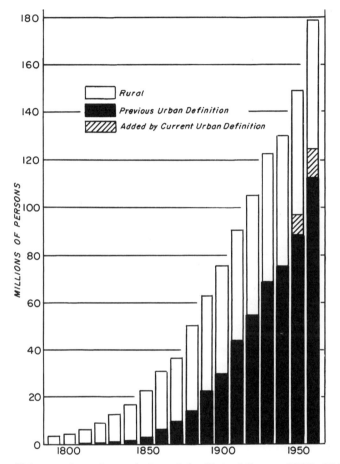

*Urban and rural population of the United States, 1790–1960.*

*The iron sinews of the railroad era in its inception, already indicating the evolving homogeneous quality of the urbanizing region.*

tremendous expansion westward. During the quarter century that followed the Civil War the mileage of American railroads trebled in length to give a significant boost to industrialization and urbanization of the country.[2] Railroads became the chief carrier of goods as well as of people. Their technological improvements—standard gauge, automatic couples, air brakes—gave a powerful impetus to the rapid growth of those centers and, what was even more important, to unifying them by connecting them with an efficient, well-integrated transportation network.

[2] Stewart H. Holbrook, *The Story of American Railroads* (New York: Crown Publishers, 1947).

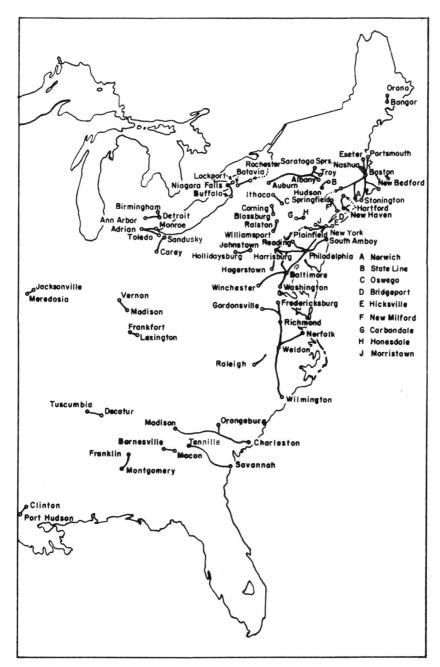

*Railroads of the Eastern United States in operation December 1840.*

The railroads of that period had a tremendous effect upon the changing function and form of the center-city as well. The location of the railroad station, usually in or around the centroid of the urban core, brought people and goods into the center-city in hitherto unknown numbers, adding greatly to the rate of growth and development of the center. However, the problems brought upon the city center were equally impressive.

The basic street layout of American cities of the prerailroad era generally followed a "grid" pattern, designed essentially around the pedestrian and horse-drawn vehicle scale. The original city centers were oriented either toward the waterfront, which formed their transportation core, or around the traditional Anglo-Saxon green, the seat of the religious and civic life of the community. The railroad station brought a new type of transportation center into their midst. The railroad lines radiating from this hub largely ignored and destroyed the established order. The weak, poorly organized and quite often corrupt administrations of urban centers were a poor match for the all-powerful railroad czars. Thus, railroad lines were laid out in the cheapest and usually most direct way towards their destination—the central railroad station—almost always ignoring the existing fabric of the community and superimposing over the old grid a completely new and foreign network of a more dynamic and curvilinear pattern.

Over the next half century this pattern exerted a major influence upon the function as well as the form of the American center-city and became one of the most important elements guiding its growth and expansion. This expansion normally followed the railroad lines, and industrial, commercial, and residential development took place along these vital lifelines to alter the original form of the city and the central urban spaces in particular. During this railroad era the urban centers of the East became great rivals, each attempting to extend its center of influence, its trade arteries, its commercial and industrial prospects and

privileges over those of other urban centers. This great interurban-center rivalry in the true tradition of American rugged individualism, raw and unmitigated, set a pattern for the shaping of the center-city that still plagues urban America today.

Industrial urban centers came into existence during this railroad era, as only through industrial enterprises could the cities hope to progress in this age of intense competition. By the end of the nineteenth century this industrial growth had freed the American economy from dependence upon European centers and from reliance upon European capital; and as foreign trade diminished in relative importance, the significance of urban centers in America mounted and their spheres of commercial and industrial influence extended over continents.[3]

On a more intimate scale, the development of intracity transportation in America also had an impact upon the growth pattern of cities and their centers. The necessity to confine the town center to an area measurable in convenient walking distances disappeared and with it the need to limit housing to dense and crowded tenements within and immediately surrounding the central urban area. The era of commuting between place of work and home began in America in all large cities in the 1860's, and in all urban centers with a population of over 50,000 in the 1880's.

The use of horse-drawn streetcars, which originally appeared on the American scene in four major cities in the 1850's, increased very rapidly and played a significant role in shaping the growth and changing the form of central urban spaces. Together with other technological improvements—bridges, telegraph, telephone, electricity, and elevators—public transportation stimulated the erection of taller buildings in central urban spaces and made possible a great concentration of business concerns in the downtown areas, thus transferring the function of these

[3] Blake McKelvey, *The Urbanization of America, 1860–1915* (New Brunswick: Rutgers University Press, 1963), p. 46.

*The electrically powered suburban railroad linked urban centers with a fast transportation system and offered an alternative to in-town living. Daft Trolley Car and Trailer, Baltimore, 1885.*

spaces from a basically town-center character to that of a centroid of metropolitan interests and activities.

The horse-drawn streetcars, however, proved inadequate in both speed and area of coverage to cope with the dynamics of American expansion and growth of urban centers, and the invention of electrically powered streetcars came almost too late to halt the increasing congestion and chaos of central spaces brought about by the railroads and the horse-drawn streetcars. It is therefore not surprising that this invention was quickly and gratefully accepted. The rapidity of this acceptance can be seen by the following comparison of the rate of expansion of electrically powered streetcars to those of horse-drawn cars: during the first

three decades of their existence horse-drawn streetcars in American urban centers utilized a little over 4,000 miles of track, while electrically powered streetcars reached the 15,000-mile mark in the very first decade.[4] Already in 1890 commuters of the ten largest cities in America transported by local carriers exceeded by 5 million the number of passengers being carried annually by steam-powered intercity railroads.

In urban centers social conditions took a dramatic spiral downward as the congestion, crowding, and poor housing became more and more deplorable during the 50-year period between 1865 and 1915. The same energy and enthusiasm that early Americans applied to conquering and civilizing the wilderness was applied with increased vigor and resolve to developing great fortunes out of the central urban areas—in the process turning them into a cultural wilderness. The enthusiastic pursuit of wealth had no counterpart in civic leadership. Without a tradition of responsibility towards the heart of the city and without adequate legal provisions, the municipal government often became corrupt and the central urban spaces became prey to unbridled land speculation. Thus, the history of the center-city was frequently one of unbalanced growth, dictated by economic factors alone and lacking in cultural and civic considerations.

The ratty social conditions within the urban centers, particularly in the older northeast section of the country, were further worsened by the waves of immigration towards the latter part of the century. This flood of unskilled, cheap labor from the rural areas of Europe had a tremendous effect upon shaping the American urban center. The creation of new neighborhoods of "little Italys," "little Polands," and "little Irelands" in the midst of the great cities revolutionized the social structure of American urban centers by splitting a relatively simple social structure

4 U.S. Bureau of the Census, Special Reports, *Street and Electric Railways* (U.S. Government Printing Office: Washington, D.C., 1907), p. 23.

*The integration through design of the new mode of public transportation into the sophisticated, urbane environment was almost total at the beginning of this century. Manhattan, 1905.*

into highly compartmentalized and socially disconnected urban nucleii. Other factors also contributed to the primitive social conditions. The police were inadequate and corrupt; city administration was full of graft and ignorance. Only social reforms of major proportions could correct such conditions.

The changes in the role of government during that time reflect a growing awareness and understanding that responsibility of government must magnify with the rate of urbanization. At the beginning of the period following the Civil War the role of government in the affairs of urban centers was limited to a few sporadic and generally meaningless gestures. One of the earliest steps in the national government's entrance into the field of urban affairs was the veterans' housing program enacted by Congress in 1868. This simple piece of housing legislation, which gave an acre or two of land to each freed Negro veteran, was rather haphazard and temporary in nature and contained no planning provisions of any kind. The purpose of this act was to aid the Negro veterans who were unable to return to their homes in the South after the war and who flocked in sizable numbers to the central urban spaces of Washington, Philadelphia, and New York. This extremely modest piece of pioneering legislation did, however, mark the entrance of the government into the field of central urban areas.

The latter part of the nineteenth century was a period of epic problems in the history of the American city, for in those days neither the local large-city government, which already was corrupt to a large degree, nor municipal laws, which were largely nonexistent, could adequately cope with the cities' growing pains. Urban planning consisted almost entirely of layouts and provisions for new public services such as water, sewage, and transportation. The greed, avarice, and ignorance that infested the larger urban communities gave rise to new slums. By the latter part of the century conditions became so unbearable that they gave rise to a progressive era marked by attempts at social and political reform.

Most of the reforms took place in the 1890's, and not until the 1940's was there a greater impetus for progressive legislation.

It is not surprising, then, that among the important social and political reforms of this period was one that authorized an investigation of slums in the larger cities (population 200,000 and over). On July 20, 1892, Congress passed a resolution to provide a sum of $20,000 for an investigation of slums by the Secretary of Labor.[5] This resolution, when it was initially introduced in the Senate, caused a great deal of debate, and there were so many objections raised on the floor that the sponsor of this bill was forced to amend it and include in it a comparison between the city slums of this country and the countries of Western Europe. The final report disclosed some shocking and rather interesting facts of slum conditions that existed in four large American cities. The study drew a sociological correlation between the presence of saloons and the number of arrests in central urban areas. It also disclosed a hitherto unknown fact, contrary to publicly held opinion in those days, that the slums in the United States were far more blighted than those of the older European cities. This report was filed away at completion and was followed by neither any governmental action aimed at improving the conditions nor any legislation.

The Congressional resolution of 1892 did, in fact, mark the first concern of the national government with urban renewal and housing in central urban spaces. This public resolution, as well as the Tenement Housing Act of 1901,[6] was passed as the result of public indignation first aroused

[5] Jack Levin, *Your Congress and American Housing* (U.S. Government Printing Office: Washington, D.C., 1952).

[6] The Tenement Housing Act of 1901, commonly referred to as the "New Law" in New York City, established the minimum 50-foot lot subdivision practice, thus outlawing the 25-foot "Railroad Plan" of 1850 and the "Dumbell Plan" of 1879, which allowed hardly any air or light inside the rooms and were responsible for the creation of some of the most inhuman living conditions. This act became a prototype for other tenement housing legislation throughout the United States.

in New York by Jacob Riis, a Danish immigrant. Riis, while working as a reporter on the *New York Sun,* syndicated sociorevolutionary articles that awoke the conscience of the country to the problems of the center-city.

As often happens in times of peace and prosperity, the human conscience lies dormant, in a state of lethargy. So, from the turn of the century until the Second World War no new legislation directed at improving the conditions of urban areas was enacted or proposed. On the local level only twelve cities had what might today resemble a housing code, and the enforcement of codes was extremely lax and ineffective. Interest in any new legislation or civic improvement in those years of overconfident urban growth completely disappeared. However, with the advent of a major crisis, the First World War, the government was forced to enter the field of urban housing. In 1918 the United States Housing Corporation was created to build, organize, and manage urban housing for the war workers. It enlisted the support and services of the leading American city planners and architects of that period. This government corporation built and managed 25 complete community projects, amounting to over 5,000 single-family dwellings in addition to apartments, dormitories, and hotels. A unique planning feature of these dwellings was the design of a single unit that was only two rooms in depth and contrasted strongly with the 100-foot-deep buildings then standard in urban subdivisions. Most of these units were sold after the war to private interests.

## 3. THE ERA OF EPIC MOVEMENT

The last 50 years of American urbanization have had the greatest impact upon central urban spaces—their shape, design, function, form, and future. This era of epic urban population explosion, motorization, auto-

*The first self-propelled individual modes of transportation were clearly designed for in-town travel, and their scale, speed, and elegance were the distinguishing mark of the refined freedom these vehicles provided. Stanley Brothers Steamer, 1897.*

*The truck soon became a necessary part of urban dynamics. While quickening the tempo of commercial growth, it also became a difficult-to-control element of movement in the city.*

mation, and eventual cybernetization has brought the American urban center to world power and influence. Prefabrication and automation have revolutionized the early twentieth-century patterns of employment, changed the function of older central urban spaces, and given birth to new ones.

The urban population in the United States almost tripled during this period, while the total population almost doubled in size. By far the greatest increase in urban population occurred in metropolitan areas, particularly in the Northeast Megalopolis. This increase of population was paralleled by the increase of educational standards to meet the new demands of increasing automation and skills. While in 1900 the percentage of illiteracy in the United States—based upon the sole criterion of inability to write, regardless of ability to read—was 10.7 percent of the population, by 1950 this figure stood at 3.2 percent. In higher education the yearly turnout of university graduates also shows a tenfold increase, from approximately 34,000 in 1907 to 408,000 in 1957.[7]

[7] U.S. Bureau of the Census, *Historical Statistics of the United States, Colonial Times to 1957* (U.S. Government Printing Office: Washington, D.C., 1960).

Transportation can be seen as a particularly dramatic force behind the changing form of central urban spaces. The combustion engine revolutionized the American urban environment in proportions that make the transformations of the nineteenth century under the impact of steam and electric power look rather insignificant. In 1913 there were already more than 1 million private automobiles registered in the United States, approximately 1 per 100 people, in addition to approximately 67,000 trucks and buses. In 1963 there were more than 68 million private automobiles, approximately 1 per 3 people, plus more than 12 million trucks and buses.[8] The great majority of these vehicles are in urban areas, in constant motion, having transformed American urban centers into uncontained quicksilver, hard to define and hard to form.

The total surfaced-road system increased almost 15-fold in mileage, from approximately 154,000 miles of surfaced roads in 1904 to 2,228,-000 miles in 1954. In 1962 the surfaced-road system within urban centers alone amounted to a total of approximately 304,000 miles.[9] These figures could be examined ad infinitum and are quoted here only to give an illustration of the orgasm of motor travel during this relatively short period of history. Examination of existing transportation conditions of urban centers will give a more detailed analysis of the effect of transportation changes of this era upon the function and space-form of the urban central space of today.

One of the greatest shortcomings in the evolution of transportation during the last 50 years has been the development of private transportation at the expense of public transportation. The transportation changes of this period brought new generators to the core of the city—bus terminals, parking lots, and air centers—which again superimposed new and foreign transportation lines over the nineteenth-century pattern of urban centers. This happened in a most haphazard fashion, with

[8] Data from U.S. Department of Commerce, Bureau of Public Roads, Washington, D.C.
[9] Ibid.

*Parking by the 1920's was already a critical problem as the fight between man and machine for central urban space began. Toledo, Ohio, east on Huron from Madison Street.*

*The development of the highway and its dramatic role in the evolution of the megalopolis is one of the great technological contributions of this era. However, while it became the lifeline of the urban galaxies, it also seriously constrained the ultimate development of central spaces by pumping unrestricted numbers of vehicles into the urban omphalos.*

*First macadam road, 1823.*

little attempt to integrate the new with the old, and with almost no comprehensive planning aimed at controlling the movement, the growth, the cohesion, and the form of central urban spaces. The resultant loss of the original form of these spaces was the direct effect of this unplanned change of transportation within as well as outside the center-city. Recognition that efficient transportation is mandatory for the healthy life of the city came too late, as urbanization took place in typically American tempo.

Social changes paralleled the changes brought about in transportation. In place of the waves of foreign immigration of an earlier era came the internal migration from rural areas to the central urban spaces. The process of assimilation of the foreign-born into American urban centers through education and social adjustment, as well as the great influx of Negro Americans from rural areas to urban centers, marks this period. Suburbanization of the cities—the flight from the center-city to new individual houses on the periphery—and the filling of city slums by rural populations was a never-ending process that only today begins to show hopes of improvement. The failure to cope with the demands of urbanization brought increased pressures upon government to act to save the central spaces from total ruin.

Thus, the role of government changed markedly during this period under the pressures of the increased tempo of urbanization, radical changes of social conditions, and new modes of transportation. However, the years following the First World War were again marked by the absence of government participation and interest in the improvement and the general welfare of the urban centers. As in the years which preceded the war, the government, reflecting the mood of the country, failed to accept the responsibilities for dealing with national urban problems.

The postwar years were noted for their rugged individualism. President Hoover symbolized this philosophy, which opposed the government's entering into any business the major purpose of which was deliberate competition with the individual citizen. This philosophy was expressed at a time when the nation was in the throes of its worst economic catastrophe. After this disaster there ensued a new social awakening and a recognition of the need for far-reaching reforms. The physical deterioration of the centers of American cities impelled the government to enter the field of urban renewal.

In studying the evolution of American urbanization it is clearly noticeable that the real comprehension of the problem of central urban spaces did not reach far beyond the preliminary stages prior to the Depression. The Depression clearly and dramatically emphasized that the role of government must increase with urbanization in order to solve national problems arising from the growth and change of central urban areas. It pointed out that these problems tend to grow in scope as the urban structure magnifies in size.

The preoccupation with housing at the expense of total central urban spaces is characterized by the formation in 1947 of the Housing and Home Finance Agency, responsible to a large degree for postwar reshaping of urban cores. The title of this authority, full of hidden implications, is worth analyzing. The first word in the title, "housing," specifically calls attention to the idea that housing, rather than total urban development, is the key problem of shaping and renewing central urban spaces.

The word "home" is one to which most Americans respond in extremely personal and emotional ways. The concept of "home is a man's castle," in true Anglo-Saxon tradition, is today even stronger in the United States than it is in England, and the idea of privacy as translated into planning in terms of an individual house on an individual lot is still a sacrosanct idea to most Americans. At the same time individual ownership is an even stronger concept deeply embedded in our economy.

*The total victory of the machine in the urban centrum.*

The result of this traditional concept is the monstrous and uncontrolled sprawl of the suburb that has grown into one of the major problems of urban planning.

In 1954 the government extended its urban renewal to nonresidential areas of central urban spaces. This was a major breakthrough in urban renewal in the United States, as the government admitted for the first time that in order to renew central urban areas the commercial, industrial, educational, cultural, civic, and recreational activities and functions must be considered alongside housing.

From this overview of the evolution of urbanization in the United States we can detect a certain pattern. The morphological cycle of the nation's social consciousness, as portrayed by social and legislative reforms, follows an undulating curve in which the height of national cultural maturity, as evidenced by interest in central urban spaces, reaches the highest points at times of national crises and catastrophes. Historically it begins with the Civil War, then drops abruptly, to come up again at the turn of the century, and to reach a certain new height during the First World War. During the times of the prosperous postwar years the curve takes a marked dip, and then suddenly shoots up and reaches hitherto unknown heights during the years of the Great Depression. From this time on only relatively small upward trends are registered. During the Second World War the rise is again significant but gradual. Following the end of the war the graph takes another dramatic upward rise that continues to this date.

These evolutionary factors of urbanization—population, transportation, social conditions, and the role of government—have shaped the conditions of the central urban spaces as they exist today. A detailed analysis of these existing conditions of the urban centers of the Northeast Megalopolis should assist in further crystallization of the problems of forming central urban spaces caused by the rapid urbanization of the United States.

## III. CREATIVE FEDERALISM: FROM SLUM CLEARANCE TO URBAN DEVELOPMENT

### 1. EMERGING ACTION

Urban and regional planning in America, as a profession and as an integral part of the function of city, county, state, and federal governments, has undergone a significant growth in the last 35 years. This growth has been paralleled by a rapid and sizable increase in the federal government's financial and technical assistance to urban areas.

The Housing Act of 1949 was the principal federal law authorizing federal assistance to slum clearance and urban redevelopment. Following its enactment, the scope of this law steadily gained momentum and by 1962 covered an area of three major assistance programs, divided as follows: Programs of Urban Assistance, Programs of Housing Assistance, and Urban Transportation Programs enacted in the Housing Act of 1961. In the past few years these programs, administered by the Housing and Home Finance Agency, have been responsible for the greatest period of housing and community improvement in the history of the United States. The Housing Act of 1965 created the Department of Housing and Urban Development, a major testimony to the national concern for shaping and controlling the development of urban America.

The actual and potential effects of this federal aid upon urban and regional planning theories and practices and upon the development of American communities are only now being examined in an attempt to comprehend this very real and intimate relationship.

The year 1932 launched the first notable federal program in the urban assistance field. The Emergency Relief and Reconstruction Act of that year created the Reconstruction Finance Corporation, which was empowered to loan government funds for low-income housing, reconstruction of urban slum areas, and the financing of self-liquidating projects. The physical deterioration of American cities, which forced the federal government to enter the field of urban reconstruction, is attested to by the Real Property Survey of 1934, which shows that one-third of all urban dwellings in the United States needed major repairs and lacked such essential elements as toilet facilities, and that only one-third were considered in good condition.[1]

The National Housing Act of 1934 created the Federal Housing Administration, a federal insurance company to insure long-term loans made by private institutions on new homes and the improvement of older homes. For example, under this act, as amended, the Federal Housing Administration, between the years 1934 and 1950, insured mortgages totaling $12.7 billion. By the mid-1930's the federal government was vitally and directly involved in the business of reviving and improving the American city. The report of President Hoover's Conference on House Building and Home Ownership was now a reality. Recommendations pertaining to the problems of slums stated that unless this problem could be met by private enterprise, there should be public participation at least to the extent of the exercise of the power of eminent domain. If the interest of business groups could not be aroused to the point where they would work out a solution of these problems through adequate measures for equity financing and large-scale operations, a further exercise of government power might be necessary.

In 1937 the United States Housing Act created the United States Housing Authority. This new federal agency provided loans and annual contributions to local public housing agencies for low-rent housing and slum-clearance projects. By 1950 this assistance provided 170,000 dwellings to low-income families.

In studying the evolution of the early federal assistance programs, it is clear that the real comprehension of the urban problem prior to the Depression did not reach far beyond very preliminary stages. The

[1] Arthur Gallion, *The Urban Pattern* (Princeton, N.J.: D. Van Nostrand, 1950), p. 138.

*Application of the urban renewal tool to America's greatest city. The over-all spatial design of Lincoln Center has acted as a catalyst for development of the adjoining area. The design of Fordham University's Lincoln Square Campus has as its predominating thought a continuation of the spatial progression of the redeveloped Center and the arrangement of new buildings to interconnect the new and existing spaces. This harmonious approach to the redevelopment of urban land is in the best tradition of creative cultural continuity. Architects: Perkins and Will.*

Depression clearly and dramatically emphasized that federal urban assistance was needed to solve national problems arising from the growth of the urban areas, and experience pointed out that these problems tend to grow in scope as the city grows. The plight of American families living in these huge urban slum areas was recognized in the provisions of the Housing Act of 1937. However, it soon became evident that a city is more than housing and that in order to control the entire growth and the orderly development of cities, new federal legislation, far in excess of the housing and slum clearance aspect of early federal urban programs, would be needed.

During the Second World War the United States was again forced to provide housing for people involved in the war effort. In 1940 the Lanham Act provided funds for 2 million dwelling units to be built during the war years. In 1942 the federal government recognized the need for coordinating all federal housing programs by creating the National Housing Agency and placing all the related agencies under this new federal body. However, the efforts of the nation were directed at winning the war, and it was not until the postwar years that the energies of the American people and of urban planners were once again directed towards revitalization and comprehensive development of urban areas.

During the years after the Second World War great debates took place in Congress, sparked by the demand to expand the urban assistance programs beyond the housing and residential concepts into the large-scale efforts to replan and redevelop the city on a comprehensive scale. These debates were bipartisan in character and were led by Senators Taft, Wagner, and Ellender. Many groups of officials and citizens spent long days on Capitol Hill trying to impress the Congress not to stand by and watch the mounting problems destroy the urban areas and pleading that the federal government accept this responsibility.

These debates and the efforts of the mayors of the larger urban centers bore fruit. Assistance in the form of federal loans and grants for

*Penn Station South, residential development, New York City. Before and after redevelopment.*

the express purpose of assisting the cities in clearing slums and rebuilding urban centers was authorized under the specific provisions of the Housing Act of 1949. These provisions were covered under various titles. Title I specifically authorized $1 billion in loans and $500 million in capital grants over a 5-year period to assist communities in slum clearance, community development, and redevelopment programs. The provisions of Title I offered municipalities financial assistance. At the same time they clearly specified the conditions, standards, and criteria under which this assistance would be given. The Act of 1949 prescribed that contracts for loans or capital grants must require that (1) the redevelopment plan be approved by the local governing body, (2) the local governing body find, among other things, that the plan conforms to a general plan of development of the locality as a whole, (3) the purchaser or lessee of the land be obligated to devote it to the uses specified in the redevelopment plan and to begin building his improvements on the land within a reasonable time. One of the major contributions of these requirements was the philosophy that the relocation of families displaced through urban redevelopment is a public responsibility and that all those displaced because of government action must be rehoused in decent, safe, and sanitary housing.

2. URBAN REDEVELOPMENT AND RENEWAL

A need existed to create a comprehensive federal program to combat slums and blight by limiting federal financial assistance to those communities willing to undertake continuing long-range programs through comprehensive planning and the enforcement of housing and building codes. The need was recognized in the broadened provisions of the Housing Act of 1954. The term "redevelopment," used in the 1949 Act and meaning the rebuilding of slums, was replaced in the Act of

*Independence Mall, Philadelphia. Before and after the restoration of this historic area.*

1954 by another term, broader and more comprehensive—"urban renewal." The term "renewal," used in conjunction with urban, is still the basic terminology, meaning the renaissance or "revivance" of physical, social, and spiritual aspects of American urban centers. The term "renewal" was borrowed from Patrick Geddes.[2]

To provide American municipalities with a methodology as well as to assure their compliance with the requirements of federal aid, Title I of the Housing Act of 1954 developed the Workable Program for Community Improvement as the chief prerequisite to urban renewal and housing assistance. Seven basic elements of the program were developed.

The first element deals with the enactment, enforcement, and periodic review of housing codes and ordinances, and is considered a preventive measure against the occurrence and spreading of slums.

The second element of the Workable Program demands that a community must have a comprehensive, current plan of development before it can qualify for federal assistance. In order initially to qualify and then continue to qualify for federal renewal and housing assistance, the community must meet the minimum requirements of having a current land-use plan, thoroughfare plan, community facilities plan, public improvements program, zoning ordinance, and map and subdivision regulations.

Detailed neighborhood analyses are required under the third element. They are aimed generally at determining the location and extent of blight by first dividing the community into a series of neighborhoods to permit a more thorough and comprehensive examination of local neighborhood conditions.

The fourth and fifth elements of the program cover administrative organization and the community's finances. A well-organized municipal

[2] Miles Colean, *Renewing Our Cities* (New York: Twentieth Century Fund, 1953), p. 28.

*Charles Center, Baltimore. Here, too, the redevelopment of this central urban space was motivated by a desire to mold significant new spaces within the city's old fabric.*

government organization is necessary for the successful effectuation of plans and wise use of federal financial assistance. Without an adequate capital improvements program the local government will not be able to schedule capital outlay in general and to meet its share of urban renewal costs in particular.[3]

The requirement for rehousing displaced families and businesses is the sixth element of this comprehensive guide and has become a major achievement of the federal program by forcing the cities into extensive housing activities.

The seventh and last element of these requirements is citizens' participation, which requires the establishment of a community citizens' advisory committee. This committee is charged with enlisting the citizens' support and with acting as the chief spokesman for the entire municipality in all urban renewal operations.

Thus, the Workable Program for Community Improvement makes urban renewal and public housing programs available only to those communities that are making satisfactory progress in developing their own community-wide programs of action aimed at the prevention as well as the elimination of urban blight.

Besides introducing the Workable Program, the Housing Act of 1954 extended urban renewal assistance to nonresidential areas. By introducing the nonresidential exception, areas that were nonresidential to start with, or those that the community planned for other than residen-

[3] Whenever a city or town undertakes an urban renewal project with federal assistance, it must provide for its share of the net project cost either in cash or in grants-in-aid. Generally, the local share amounts to one-third of the net cost in communities of 50,000 or less and one-fourth of the net for larger cities. Sometimes the state in which the community is located contributes one-half of the local share, as is the case in New York, Connecticut, Pennsylvania, and Massachusetts. However, these states are the exception and not the rule; in the majority of the states the localities have to assume their full share. This share, however, does not necessarily have to be in cash, but can also be in non-cash grants-in-aid, which include the cost of public improvements directly benefiting the urban renewal project area.

tial re-use, could also benefit from the capital grant funds as long as they did not exceed 10 percent of total federal grant funds. This figure was later amended to 30 and subsequently to 35 percent, indicating a trend towards a more comprehensive city-wide renewal philosophy. This was a major breakthrough in the urban renewal program, for by passing this legislation the Congress admitted for the first time that commercial, industrial, educational, civic, and recreational activities must be considered alongside housing in order to renew cities. The renewal program was thus recognized as being separate from the slum clearance program, for although they are often coincidental, they do not necessarily overlap each other.

One of the most significant contributions of the Housing Act of 1954 to urban planning in America was Section 701, which established the Urban Planning Assistance Program. This professional, comprehensive planning legislation did more to encourage such planning in the United States than almost any other measure. The urban planning assistance and urban renewal programs deserve particularly close and critical scrutiny. Section 701 of the Housing Act of 1954 authorized the Urban Renewal Administration of the Housing and Home Finance Agency to make planning grants to state and local governments in order to assist them in solving planning problems, facilitate comprehensive planning for urban development, and encourage local governments to establish and improve their planning staffs. Under this program, which is directed at smaller communities (with a maximum population of 50,000), federal grant-in-aid amounts to two-thirds of the costs of planning; the nonfederal share of costs is in the form of cash and services. The federal grants are made through appropriate state planning agencies.[4] Official

[4] State planning agencies that administer this program vary greatly in composition as well as in actual name. In Alabama the agency which is responsible for administering the 701 Program is the State Planning and Industrial Development Board; in California, Department of Finance; in Kentucky, Department of Commerce; in Louisiana, Department of Public Works; in Maryland, State Planning Department; in Minnesota,

state, metropolitan, and regional planning agencies can apply directly to a regional office of the Department of Housing and Urban Development.[5] In some cases the state assists the locality through cash or services in providing for the nonfederal share of the project.

The original appropriation for this project was $20 million. By 1961 it had increased to $75 million, and it now stands at $230 million. The planning work that is eligible under this assistance program covers all the basic essentials of urban planning. These include survey and analysis of population, economy, physiography, land use, transportation, community facilities, and urban design studies. The preparation of the comprehensive plan of development must, in order to satisfy the requirements of the program, have a clear and definite statement of community goals and policies in addition to the land use, highway, and community facilities plans. Preparation of local programs leading to the implementation of the comprehensive development plan includes the capital improvements program, zoning and subdivision regulations, and assistance in preparation of housing and construction codes. Coordinating and administrative activities include coordination of plans of local, regional, state, and federal agencies, and local public urban-planning education programs.

The cost of updating and maintaining current basic community planning data is also an eligible activity under the 701 Program. Various specific planning studies not eligible in the early years of the program

---

Department of Business Development; in New Mexico, State Planning Office; in Texas, State Department of Health. In states where no state planning agency exists, the federal government may accept some instrumentality of the state government to be designated by the Governor as the state planning agency. In this way the state university has often been so designated, as is the case in the states of Arizona, Arkansas, and Indiana.

[5] The United States is divided into seven regions, with the regional offices of the Department of Housing and Urban Development located in New York City, Philadelphia, Atlanta, Chicago, Fort Worth, San Francisco, and Santurce, Puerto Rico.

are now eligible for federal financial assistance; to mention but a few: urban transportation studies, planning of central business districts, open-space land plans, and park and recreation plans. Specific architectural and engineering studies are not allowed under the provisions of this program, since the main objective is the development of comprehensive plans leading to sound over-all urban development rather than of individual projects.

In 1956 the concept of urban renewal was again expanded with the authorization to assist financially the families and businesses in meeting the costs of moving caused by urban renewal. In addition, the project concept of urban renewal was greatly expanded by the authorization of federal financial advances for the preparation of general neighborhood renewal plans. In cities where the planning areas were found to be so large and contiguous as to be beyond the economic feasibility of execution as a single project, it now became possible to schedule the renewal process of up to ten years in time. This more comprehensive approach was further extended by the creation of the Community Renewal Program in 1959, which authorized grants to assist communities in analyzing urban blight on a community-wide scale, to identify available resources, and to formulate a local policy-action program to eliminate the blight conditions before they occur. Together with general planning activities permitted under the Urban Planning Assistance Program, the activities allowed under the Community Renewal Program have given American communities an opportunity hitherto unknown to plan their future comprehensively, intelligently, and in a farsighted manner.

The federal share of the Community Renewal Program activities usually amounts to two-thirds of the total costs, the remainder being borne by the locality in terms of cash or services. The key elements of this program are economic analysis of the community to arrive at the economic basis for all future renewal activities along with a drafting of

*Constitution Plaza,*
*Hartford.*

*Penn Center, Philadelphia. The railroad tracks, 40 feet above street level on a brick structure called the "Chinese Wall" by generations of Philadelphians, was demolished and replaced by the modern buildings, pedestrian esplanades, and landscaping. Railroad commuter station and bus terminal form an integral part of this complex.*

*Tiber Island, residential development, Washington, D.C. Architects: Keyes, Lethbridge, and Condon.*

goals for community renewal and of a timetable for planning and co-ordinating all renewal activities. Modern computers have been employed in many community renewal program operations recently and have assembled total records of urban land-parcel characteristics that under manual systems would be prohibitive in cost.

The Housing Act of 1961 further liberalized the provisions of urban renewal by shifting more of the financial burden away from the localities to the shoulders of the federal government. Today three-fourths of the net project cost is paid by the federal government, which means that the city has only to put up one dollar out of every four dollars spent on urban renewal. This act also recognized the scope of urban renewal problems in America by doubling previous authorizations to a total of $4 billion, and it established the Open-Space Land Program and the Mass Transportation Program, as well as greatly liberalizing many housing programs.

The Open-Space Land Program was passed in answer to the concern for preserving open spaces in our congested urban areas. President

*Columbia Plaza, residential development, Washington, D.C. Architects: Keyes, Lethbridge, and Condon.*

Kennedy expressed this concern in the following words: "Land is the most precious resource in the metropolitan area. The present patterns of haphazard suburban development are contributing to a tragic waste in the use of a vital resource now being consumed at an alarming rate. Open space must be reserved to provide parks and recreation, conserve water and other natural resources, prevent building in undesirable locations, prevent erosion and floods, and avoid the wasteful extension of public service. Open land is also needed to provide reserves for future residential development, to protect against undue speculation, and to make it possible for state and regional bodies to contribute to control the rate and character of community development."

Recognizing the urgent need to provide land in the cities for recreational, conservation, scenic, and historical purposes, the Congress enacted Title VII of the Housing Act of 1961 with the express purpose of assisting communities, regions, and states in providing this open-space land that otherwise would be financially impossible for the municipalities to acquire. In order to be eligible for federal assistance, land to be acquired

under this Act must be located in an urban or urbanized area.[6] Federal grants were authorized for between 20 and 30 percent of the purchase price of the land. As in other federal urban assistance programs, the community interested in participating must meet a set of urban planning requirements, the most important being that the area to be purchased must be important to the execution of the comprehensive plan and also that the maximum of open-space land is being preserved by the community through zoning and other regulations.

Under Section 303 of the Housing Act of 1961, Congress appropriated $25 million for mass-transportation demonstration projects to assist in implementing urban transportation plans, research, and testing of new ideas and new methods for improving mass transportation systems. These grants were not to exceed two-thirds of the cost. By authorizing this expenditure the Congress has finally recognized one of the greatest dilemmas plaguing the American city. There is no urban center in the United States where the streets are not congested with automobiles. The rapidly increasing urban population, the use and ownership of motor vehicles, and the intensity of land-use further increase traffic congestion and make provisions for adequate parking for private automobiles in the larger urban hubs a near impossibility.

The development of efficient mass transportation systems well integrated into comprehensive urban plans has long been recognized by professional American urban and regional planners. The entrance of the federal government into this field offers the first ray of hope for an actual solution in the not-too-distant future.

[6] This definition generally follows the Bureau of Census definition for a standard metropolitan statistical area or an urbanized area. The urban population in America is rapidly increasing. In 1910 40 percent of the United States population lived in urban areas. Between 1950–1960, 97 percent of the population growth occurred in urban areas. By 1960, 70 percent of Americans lived in urban areas; and the prediction for 1980 is that 80 percent of all the population in the United States will be urban.

3. A NEW CHARTER

The legislative innovations of 1965 attempt for the first time to come
to grips with the complex and interdependent nature of urban problems,
as exemplified by the wide, interrelated range of programs authorized by
the Housing and Urban Development Act of 1965. Megalopolitan development, not only in the Northeast but also in the Midwest, along the
West Coast, and other areas, was tackled by the Eighty-ninth Congress
in passing legislation establishing the Department of Housing and Urban
Development and in authorizing $8,243,000,000 over a four-year period
for programs of the Housing and Urban Development Act. The dynamics
of urban growth and the need for greater emphasis upon social problems
and the process of shaping central urban spaces were recognized by
President Johnson when he defined these problems in his message on the
cities: "The problem is people and the quality of the lives they lead. We
want to build not just housing units but neighborhoods; not just to construct schools, but to educate children; not just to raise income, but to
create beauty and end the poisoning of our environment. We must extend the range of choices available to all our people so that all, and not
just the fortunate, can have access to decent homes and schools, to
recreation and to culture."

Many of the program innovations of the Act of 1965 reflect the
principle that social conditions determine urban design and that urban
design shapes social conditions. The broader recognition among planners of the need for a comprehensive interaction of all national programs is also evident in such related programs as those contained in the
Civil Rights and Economic Opportunity acts of 1964, the medicare bill,
the voting rights bill, and the education bills.

The expansion of the existing housing programs for low- and
moderate-income families, the elderly, and the handicapped, along with
the rent supplement program (initially delayed by lack of funding)

*Boston, Government Center. To the right is a view of the initial construction of this new center as depicted below.*

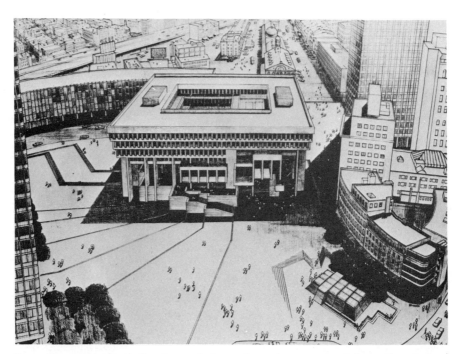

form the major contributions of the enlarged concept of "creative federalism" of the mid-1960's. The so-called "flexible formula" of the Housing Act of 1965 authorized the Public Housing Administration to extend financing to housing units whether they be in good condition or require rehabilitation, for as short or long a term as necessary, from private owners or nonprofit organizations. This provision enables local housing authorities to provide low-income housing much more rapidly than was previously possible through new construction alone. It also provides new tools for solving special social and community problems in encouraging conservation and improvement of existing residential neighborhoods, thus assisting in the elimination of economic ghettos. Thus, the public housing program, which since its inception in 1937

has provided housing for approximately 2.5 million people in 600,000 units, was now authorized to provide 240,000 additional housing units in the short span of four years.

The Urban Renewal authorizations of the Act of 1965 amounted to $2,900,000,000 for capital grants and $450,000,000 for rehabilitation loans, the latter reflecting a growing emphasis upon the importance of the rehabilitation process of central urban spaces. The planning requirements for the Urban Renewal Program were strengthened again. Further steps aimed at making the urban renewal effort more effective were the provisions for much-needed research activities, the study of housing and building codes, zoning ordinances, tax policies, and development standards.

The Urban Planning Assistance grants were increased from $105 million in 1954 to $230 million in 1965, and 5 percent of these funds can be used for research studies and demonstration projects, for the development of planning and design methods, and for the advancement of comprehensive urban planning. The Act of 1965 also permits planning grants to be made to representatives of metropolitan areas or urban regions, thus assisting in solving metropolitan and regional planning problems. These grants, presently limited to two-thirds of the cost of the planning work, may now be used to solve megalopolitan problems and offer a new tool for shaping megalopolitan urban centers.

The preservation of historic structures in central urban spaces was given token recognition in the Act of 1965 by permitting the cost of relocating within an urban renewal area of a structure determined by the renewal agency to be of historic value. This is neither preservation nor conservation.

Urban design was further strengthened through the innovations of the Act of 1965 by enlarging the Open-Space Land Program to include urban beautification and improvement and by significantly increasing federal authorizations to a total of $235 million.

These accomplishments of the 1965 legislation were a response to President Johnson's challenging words: "Between now and the end of this Century our urban population will double. City land will double. In the next 35 years, we must literally build a second America—putting in place as many houses, schools, apartments, parks, and offices as we have built through all the time since the Pilgrims arrived on these shores."

## IV. THE CONVERGING STREAMS: THE NEED FOR BALANCE AND UNITY

### 1. THE INVISIBLE DESIGN AND THE VISIBLE PLAN

The factors that today limit the design and shaping of urban centers are the result of the forces of urbanization over the last century. This evolutionary process is characterized by a unique economic expansion that superimposed a new pattern over cities originally designed for an entirely different economy, population, and urban way of life. This largely unplanned and unrestricted expansion along the lines of least resistance, without attempts to integrate the new with the old to preserve the necessary cultural continuity, is responsible for the existing conditions in the hubs of urban America.

The degree of urban design controls required to resist and counteract uncontrolled processes in shaping these spaces is occupying the attention of all who are committed to the creation of a vibrant, animated, and truly inspirational man-made environment. The search for more meaningful and effective ways of planning and designing urban spaces for the millions of megalopolitan citizens leads in many directions. The need for a unified multidisciplinary approach in solving the many-faceted urban problems through a thorough reappraisal of educational methodology and philosophy is bringing balance and unity to hitherto highly compartmentalized and often uncommunicative branches of human knowledge. Recently there has been a growing recognition on the part of leading educators of an increasing need to reorganize the American university's activities in education and scholarly research from the traditional subject-matter-oriented studies to synoptic and comprehensive area-wide programs. This philosophy is being applied particularly to the fields of urban planning, design, and research and also to the general programs in urban and regional studies. This field, with its chief aim—

"Study of the City and of Man in the Contemporary Urban Environment"—is only today becoming a catalytic, unifying force in American higher education.

Urban studies, as we are aware today, evolved out of an early interest in the fields of social and political institutions and reforms caused by industrialization and urbanization in the latter part of the nineteenth century. As early as 50 years ago urban studies, originally referred to as civics, were already foreseen by Patrick Geddes in England as the progressive revolutionary science of the twentieth century. Disturbed by the superficial attention paid to social development in the process of shaping man's urban environment, he saw urban studies as the meaningful and unifying science of this era. In viewing the contributions and struggles of specific branches of human knowledge as they emerged during certain historical periods, he envisioned urban studies as playing the same significant role in twentieth-century life as did astronomy in the Renaissance and geology and biology in the nineteenth century. By his awareness of the dynamic quality of synoptic urban studies, he foresaw the displacement of eclectic and superficial urban planning concepts of the turn of the century by vibrant and dynamic new concepts as the result of a synoptic approach, just as geocentric astronomy and the nonevolutionist geology or biology were replaced by more dynamic concepts.[1] He particularly attacked the uncreative and academic use of older, static planning concepts in attempting to solve the problems of the twentieth century.

The theories of pioneer English town planners have had a great influence upon shaping American thoughts on this subject. The work of Patrick Geddes, Raymond Unwin, and Ebenezer Howard laid the base for American urban-planning principles, and much of their philosophy and breadth of vision have seen fruition here. Of all the early city planning pioneers in England, it is Geddes who has had the greatest influence upon

[1] Patrick Geddes, *Cities in Evolution* (London: Williams & Norgate, 1949), p. 100.

American urban planning. Geddes' deep philosophical approach to urban planning at the beginning of the twentieth century revolutionized the nineteenth-century idea of town planning and, in giving it proper social, economic, and political perspective, led to the development of modern planning in America. A synoptic view of all phases of the life of the city and an insistence that physical planning must be based upon and integrated with social, economic, and political planning are for Geddes the essence of design. Thoughts expressed by him on the role of citizens and the responsibilities of professionals in the planning process are only today beginning to be accepted widely outside the planning profession.

One of the basic thoughts developed by Geddes is the need for the active participation by citizens in community planning activities in a democratic society. Education for citizenship, or as he terms it, "civic renewal," is necessary to arouse among members of the community the kind of civic enthusiasm and vital interest in urban planning that he considers a prerequisite to the development and implementation of plans. The thesis that plans will succeed only when professional planners and public officials have the backing of the people is an increasingly recognized principle of planning and shaping American urban centrums.

The influence of English thought has been so strong that it has tended to diminish the influence of Continental theories and experiments. The investigations and studies of Camillo Sitte of Austria at the turn of the century are less understood than the theories of Patrick Geddes of England. Yet the ideas of Sitte, particularly relating to the spatial concepts of urban design, are of particular interest and value to the planner of today. In fact, Camillo Sitte's contribution to the understanding of the art of city design has widely been recognized in Europe, but his artistic concerns have had relatively little influence upon the generally rather pragmatically oriented urban planning theories of the United States.

In attempting to alter the amorphous nature of the megalopolis—to give it human scale, form-coherence, and significant urban spaces—

Sitte's philosophies and theories, as well as the accomplishments of other great city designers of the past, need constant re-examination. Just as technology in itself does not provide an answer to the solution of the problems of the modern city, neither in themselves do philosophy, sociology, economics, political science, or cybernetics. The artistic, philosophic, and historical concerns—the fundamental laws of city-building as understood by Sitte—should be considered equally important. Only then, as he wrote, will the city center once again become a place fully expressive of the dignity of man and the central urbanscape as inspirational to human senses as the landscape.[2]

Social and economic problems during this century have become of such paramount importance that they have overshadowed the investigations into the field of urban design. Since governmental action of one kind or another is necessary to control the building and rebuilding of central urban spaces, adequate architectural and urban design controls must be developed. As of this time there are almost no such controls that would prevent the spread of obsolescence and architectural disorder permeating the city center and that would give the integral parts of the city adequate form-coherence.

The control of building design and of building obsolescence in central urban spaces in America has as yet remained almost untouched. The only central urban areas where it is usually possible to control to any degree the architectural design of buildings is in the urban renewal areas —and even there the controls are in their infancy. The American center-city stands as a living proof that uncontrolled architectural design results in unsatisfactory urban design and in insensitive, chaotic, and uncivilized urban physical environment. Coherence of forms in urban centrums is almost entirely lacking. Walking past newly constructed buildings in a typical urban omphalos can be compared to an experience

[2] Camillo Sitte, *The Art of Building Cities* (New York: Reinhold Publishing Corp., 1945).

*India Wharf, Boston, built in 1805 by the architect Charles Bulfinch. One of the landmarks of the maritime capital of New England and a monument of unquestioned historic significance, this building was demolished unnecessarily in 1962 in an urban renewal area. No attempt was made to preserve and enhance the space which it originally dominated.*

of flipping through the pages of architectural magazines—each building, regardless of its own intrinsic architectural merit, is utterly unrelated to its surroundings and tends also to destroy the street as an urban form. Since, according to Plato, objects in themselves have no meaning, the quality of relatedness being the parent of reality, the architecture of such structures is indeed devoid of much meaning, and in these terms these buildings may indeed be considered as unreal.

It is sometimes difficult to comprehend the emotional reaction to the idea of design controls. Such controls are considered by many as an arbitrary violation of the rights and civil liberties guaranteed by the Constitution. Although there are sporadic attempts at architectural controls, they have not been based upon an over-all design policy and plan or backed by legislative provisions or enforcement, and thus are often ineffectual.

In recent years urban design failures in urban renewal have been recognized, and an attempt is being made to encourage communities to dispose of downtown land to developers on the basis of architectural competitions in the hope that the best architectural talent will be employed in rebuilding the center-city. The Urban Renewal Administration is known for its emphasis upon the need for good urban design. "Unless [a city] has developers who also recognize the importance of good design, developers who employ architects who know and practice good design, their plans will result in more monuments to sterility, negativity, and futility."[3] Achieving good urban design in city centrums through architectural competitions is a relatively new practice in the United States. Competitions conducted in recent years in such cities as Washington and Boston, in connection with urban renewal activities of central urban spaces, have proven themselves successful in obtaining

[3] William L. Slayton, "Disposition, Development and Design," Housing and Home Finance Agency Release (U.S. Government Printing Office: Washington, D.C., 1962).

*A growing governmental and private recognition of the need of cultural continuity through integration of new construction with historic landmarks. These design sketches are part of a siting study for a new office building in Boston. Architects: Perkins and Will.*

outstanding individual architecture, if not outstanding urban design, and have thus initiated a new trend.

Thus, the lack of comprehension of the concept or of the process of design in the development of urban and regional areas is due to a general shortage of qualified planners and designers, lack of adequate research, too great a demand for practical work, and a vacuum of a theoretical base. These factors are interdependent with the legal and political limitations in effectuating the development of central urban spaces.

## 2. CONTROLS FOR MACRO-URBANISM

A reappraisal of the potential of existing legal tools is necessary for the implementation of the synoptic design concept in megalopolitan conditions. Existing regulatory and enforcement powers such as the traditional police power and the power of eminent domain, as they relate to zoning, urban renewal, and other elements of comprehensive planning, should be used with more skill and imagination.

While under the enforcement or police-power provisions the state can deny the property owner specific use of his land if it is contrary to the public purpose, under the power of eminent domain the state can actually condemn the property through a due process of law and pay for this forced sale a price based upon a fair-market value. Fair-market value is determined by the courts on the basis of testimony of impartial private appraisers and witnesses representing the owner and the community. In the United States a police-power provision is used mostly in enforcing zoning regulations, and the power of eminent domain is exercised by the local government in condemning property in urban renewal activities, highway construction, and enforcement of housing codes.

Some very significant changes have taken place during the last three decades through a broader and more comprehensive interpretation of these powers. Originally confined to public health, safety, and general welfare, the use of police power later was enlarged to include such matters as public convenience and public comfort. Traffic laws and laws excluding obnoxious uses of land have been made possible under that interpretation. For a long time it was generally thought that the courts would not recognize the people's esthetic environmental needs as falling under these provisions. In more recent times, however, the United States Supreme Court declared that esthetic considerations are important to health and general welfare, thus giving a ray of hope for a still broader application of these powers to new tools designed to assist in creating a more human and more dignified urban environment.[4]

The need for urban-development legislation was clearly outlined almost 30 years ago in the work of Eliel Saarinen, a European-born American architect-city planner. His opinions are particularly profound as his intimate knowledge of European planning practices, combined with a deep personal and professional experience in America, make his evaluations particularly relevant.

Saarinen's thesis for the need of new "civic" legislation was based on the assumption that most existing urban ordinances were written around concepts that were invalidated by new means of transportation and new conditions of urban life. He recognized the artificiality of political boundaries as they affect comprehensive urban planning and the shaping of metropolitan cores. Most cities in the United States have long outgrown their municipal boundaries, creating economic and planning problems of epic proportions. As an example, the metropolitan area of the nation's capital covers parts of two states, in addition to the District of Columbia, each with a separate political and legislative system, as well as a multitude of municipal and county governments more or less independent to pursue their own development as they see fit. It is not

[4] Berman vs. Parker, 348 U.S. 26, 75 Sup. Ct. 98, 99 L. Ed. 27 (1954).

*The Harral-Wheeler Mansion, Bridgeport, Connecticut, built in 1846. Architect: Alexander Jackson Davis. Midnineteenth-century American experimentation with Gothic revival. Masterfully executed, this building was preserved into the midtwentieth century. Entrusted to the city, it became a major political campaign issue and was ultimately destroyed despite efforts of the Bridgeport Historical Society to preserve it.*

surprising that progress in the comprehensive development of this important urban entity is extremely slow, being based mainly on voluntary cooperation between municipal, county, state, and national agencies. As almost always occurs in cases of uncoordinated "voluntary cooperation," there is chaos, duplication of effort, resultant stalemate, little actual cooperation, and still less planning progress. The basic structural elements of an urbanized region as well as transportation, utilities, and open space should be placed under a strong, fully empowered regional planning authority to ensure unifying fiscal and legal land-use controls. Such a policy would assist in furthering the orderly development of the metropolitan area.

At the present time communities have little control over land-price matters. Zoning, instead of preventing land speculation, has actually put a premium on the downtown districts and tends to inflate the price of land. The value of central urban land climbs constantly and makes the creation of humane urban environment increasingly difficult. Uncontrolled land speculation, given full freedom, makes city expansion, urban renewal, and comprehensive city development equally impossible. Saarinen proposed that legislative authorities undertake measures to bring land-price under the municipal government's control. Urban renewal's relative success can be traced mainly to the fact that it is the first legislative measure that attempts to deal with this problem; and although not entirely successful in preventing speculation, it places the land of central spaces to be renewed under controls.

The need for an extension of power in the field of land condemnation through broadened interpretation of the power of eminent domain is constantly being recognized and met by communities. What was originally applied only to unsafe and blighted structures in central urban areas is being extended to transportation routes and public land, for example, park, play, and other open-space land areas. A plan of development is slowly becoming a powerful instrument, and is being recognized more often in courts as a basis for condemnation activities. Thus, Saarinen's recommendation to bring the law of condemnation up to the level of the demands of metropolitan planning is beginning today to take place.[5]

In analyzing the interrelated limiting factors of the center-city, and in synthesizing legislative and design elements in their effect upon central urban spaces, it is worthwhile to remember the words of another outstanding European planner, Tadeusz Tołwiński: "The monumental squares of Paris, Versailles, the old part of Berlin, the old Petersburg—those are examples of the effect of the urban plan working together with proper legislative measures in shaping the city. . . . This harmony between the legal and the technical method of shaping the city disappeared at a time when only close and integrated joint action could lead to positive results. This can particularly well be seen at the turn of the nineteenth century, that is, during a period of almost total fall of urban culture."[6] Today the world is experiencing a great expansion of urban population. It is too early to tell whether this will lead to still greater urban chaos in the heart of the city and still worse slums in central urban spaces, or to a period of concentration of urban culture hitherto unknown in the history of mankind. Our culture can afford nothing short of the recognition of the dignity of man through creative urban design and of his maturity through significant urban legislation.

The sciences in general, and technology and cybernetics in particular, are advancing at a faster pace than the humanities and the arts. It is therefore very tempting to find the answers to urban planning problems in those terms rather than in a more human, balanced approach. The new science of cybernetics has already had an impact upon the

[5] Eliel Saarinen, *The City: Its Growth, Its Decay and Its Future* (New York: Reinhold Publishing Corp., 1943), p. 321.

[6] Tadeusz Tołwiński, *Urbanistyka* (Warsaw: Trzaska, Evert, i Michalski, 1947), Vol. I, p. 26.

science of urban planning, but it is neither a panacea nor a cure-all. Among the outstanding American thinkers of today, Lewis Mumford stands in the front ranks of those who recognize the value of human, social, and artistic fundamentals of urban ecology. He disagrees with the concept held by some professional planners and European scholars who profess belief in the self-direction of the organic life of the center-city without the need of regulatory powers.[7] This philosophy of planning has been more or less practiced in the United States in the past and has to a large degree been responsible for the lack of organization, order, and form-coherence of central urban spaces. Comparisons of the structure of the center-city with living biological organisms tend to overlook the fact that these organisms are highly coordinated by the power that created them and that some sort of power is necessary to create an order that would prevent utter chaos and lawlessness in the life of the city.

Mumford categorically states that no "profit-oriented, pressure-dominated" economy can cope with the mammoth job of rebuilding the centers of our cities and that the chief responsibility of the heart of the city is the welfare and the culture of man.[8] He compares the problem of urban renewal of central areas with one of human procreation and states that if humanity would direct as much enthusiasm to a renaissance of central urban spaces as it does to its biological reproduction, "public service would take precedence over private profit and public funds would be available for the building and rebuilding of villages, neighborhoods, cities and regions." "The building materials for a new urban order . . . are at hand. But the possibility that they will continue to be misused and perverted by the existing political systems is high. The prospect of a massive extension of our present mechanico-electronic fa-

[7] H. B. Reichow, *Organische Städtebaukunst* (Braunschweig: B. I. Georg Westerman Verlag, 1948).

[8] Lewis Mumford, *The City in History* (New York: Harcourt, Brace and World, 1961), pp. 567–575.

*Bushnell Plaza Apartment Towers in central Hartford is a statement of the new and the historically significant mutually enhanced through a harmonious relationship. Architect: I. M. Pei.*

cilities, without any change or social pressure . . . remains ominous.
. . . The thinkers who will do for this organic and human conception
what Galileo, Bacon and Descartes did for our now insufficient and even
dangerously outmoded concepts of science and technology have long
been at work. But it may need another century or two before their contributions will have dethroned our Cybernetic Deities and restored to the
center of our existence the images and forces and purposes of life."[9]


## 3. THE NEW URBAN ENTREPRENEURS

The renewal of urban centrums through a partnership between free
enterprise and the public authorities creates unique problems and opportunities. Generally speaking, the partnership is designed to work in
the following way: the government provides the power of eminent domain, the financial subsidies, the organization, coordination, and control,
while private enterprise supplies the lion's share of the investment capital, which amounts to almost six times the amount of government capital
grants.[10] Although there are a great many areas—cultural, economic,
and other—in which their interests are coincidental, this partnership is
basically complementary in nature—each side providing a different set
of contributions towards the common goal of developing American central urban spaces.

The chief advantage of this partnership to the private associate in
the venture is the ability to redevelop central urban land at a cost much
lower than if he had to buy, clear, and develop the land at his own

[9] *Ibid.*

[10] The ratio of private redevelopers' investment to public investment as based on 479
projects in which some or all land was disposed of as of June 1963 was 5.96 dollars
for every dollar of public capital grants. William Slayton, *Report on Urban Renewal.*
Statement before the Subcommittee on Housing, U.S. House of Representatives (U.S.
Government Printing Office: Washington, D.C., 1963).

expense, as well as the fact that his investment is safeguarded through comprehensive planning and controls. Thus through urban renewal the investor-developer is able to undertake projects in city centrums which otherwise would not be economically feasible.

The local government benefits from this partnership mainly through a general reduction in the expensive services that the municipality must provide to all blighted central urban areas, greater increased tax revenues from the land that has been redeveloped, and an injection of economic boosters into the organism of the community in the form of private and public investments.[11]

The advantages to the national partner are not quite so clearly defined or so concrete as they are to the community and to private enterprise, but they are even greater in their scope and potential effects. Since the economic life of an urban country is dictated by the conditions of each and all central urban areas, the national economy derives great benefit from the stimulation of local economy through renewal and increased building activity in the center-city.

The cultural, social, and human benefits common to all parties involved are obvious. However, it must be stressed, without drawing a detailed classification of all groups and forces involved in the renewal of central urban spaces, that the above-outlined partnership is neither clearly defined nor the relationship rigid and unchanging. Quite the contrary, the character and pattern of this great association is constantly in a state of change and reappraisal by all sides concerned.

Both private enterprise and the public authorities agree on the need for revitalizing and rebuilding the centers of towns and cities; where private enterprise often differs from the general aim is in the methods that should be employed. Among the organized groups that

[11] Comparison of assessed valuations of land before and after urban renewal shows 427% increase based on information from 403 projects in which redevelopment was started or is completed. *Ibid.*

have long opposed public subsidies for urban renewal is the Chamber of Commerce of the United States, although almost all of the local Chambers of Commerce in American cities have cooperated with and supported urban renewal of their downtown.[12] The vital interest of the national business community in the future of urban areas is exemplified by the creation in 1965 by the Chamber of Commerce of the United States of a task force for the study of urban problems. This task force, which consists of 100 top-level industrialists, will attempt to arrive at recommendations for modernizing political institutions, speeding up social progress, and improving the shaping of central urban spaces. This participation of American business in establishing goals and objectives for urban planning and development is an important landmark in the evolving response of the business community to comprehensive urban development.

Local opposition in certain parts of the country to the renewal of central urban spaces can be divided between those whose political philosophy opposes public "interference" in the "sovereign" affairs of the community and those—usually less numerous but more vocal—who fear controls as limiting their own profit potential. The influence of those opposing the local urban renewal effort has often been significant. Many communities, in particular smaller ones, have not initiated renewal programs in their downtown because of this opposition, and others have had limited success because of the pressures exerted by these groups.

Among the criticisms of downtown renewal programs that can be substantiated, the most significant is that they are inadequate in scope and insufficient in financial resources to be able to renew effectively all central urban areas. Although this has to be recognized as a gigantic long-term goal, renewal appropriations for central urban areas have up

12 *The Impact of Federal Urban Renewal and Public Housing Subsidies,* Chamber of Commerce of the United States (Washington, D.C., 1964).

to now been passed only as short-term plans. The chief aim of the long-term plan is to establish a long-range over-all perspective that can be used to guide future growth of a community through a general and relatively reliable set of predictions and assumptions. Such a comprehensive plan would provide a framework of perspective against which short-term plans can be developed and judged. The development of general comprehensive plans of development falls into this range. During the last ten years cities have had a tendency to develop plans for the year 1980 or the year 2000. It is difficult to predict whether the rapid changes in urban life will be offset by improved urban planning methodology, thus to force either an extension or a reduction of this rather arbitrary time schedule.

Urban renewal's success in arousing public enthusiasm and support has to a large extent been based upon the fact that it is a program of action and of visible results. The slow and difficult acceptance of comprehensive community planning on the part of the general public as well as public authorities has been due to the fact that until urban renewal the aims of planning rested entirely in the future and were removed from the pressing and mounting everyday problems of central urban spaces.

However, it is this very limitation of being associated only with short-term planning, and with specific projects rather than with total center-city development, that has hampered urban renewal. Such experimental activities of the American urban renewal effort can achieve only a limited impact as long as the number of acres of renewed land is outstripped by the number of acres of central urban spaces which are becoming blighted and decayed. It is estimated that approximately three times as many dwelling units in urban areas are falling into substandard conditions as are being eliminated.[13]

Another problem and limitation of urban renewal to date has been

[13] Boston Municipal Research Bureau, *Charting the Future of Urban Renewal,* IV (Boston, 1958).

the dominance of bureaucratic regulations and a tendency to a division of power and fragmentation of authority. The highway program is by far the most glaring example of this unfortunate lack of adequate coordination. Since highway appropriations have in the past been and still are far in excess of urban renewal subsidies, the highway planner has been placed in the position of a dictator of the location and design of the transportation system in and around the center-city. Having been granted the power and the money, he has in the past ignored the comprehensive plan of the community and has cut many an American city center in half or strangled its growth by placing a chastity belt—a circumferential highway—around it, thus making the effectuation of plans obsolete overnight.

Probably one of the greatest weaknesses of the use of the urban renewal tool has been the failure on the part of cities to apply it in a way that would encourage creative architecture and good urban design, except for a few notable examples in larger cities. Although urban renewal gives the communities the tools with which they could obtain that goal, most cities and towns have to date not taken advantage of this unique opportunity. In the field of public housing in central urban areas in particular the cry of urban renewal antagonists that "old slums are being replaced by new ones" has some truth in it. Brick or metal curtain walls enclose in some cities barracks-like apartment houses of inhuman scale, devoid of architectural qualities. Into these towers are placed families from single-family dwellings of the older areas. Although substituting dwelling units with adequate sanitary facilities for slums, these new quarters neither express the needs of the people nor do much to renew their life socially, culturally, or educationally.

In the field of the preservation of America's historic architectural and urban design heritage, which exists in the form of great and exciting individual buildings and entire sections of towns and cities in the Northeast Megalopolis, little has been accomplished by urban renewal

*Brutal destruction of existing urban fabric through the construction of an interstate highway through East Providence, Rhode Island. No attempt is made to respect the scale of the city or to provide even a setback or screen planting, the result being to give the impression of driving through the backyards of houses.*

THE WHITE HOUSE

WASHINGTON

October 15, 1962

Dear Bernie:

I would like to tell you how pleased Mrs. Kennedy and I are with the preliminary architectural studies of Lafayette Square.

I have been reflecting on the significance of this work, not only in the terms of the importance of it to the environs of the White House and our capital, but to what it means in a broader sense to other cities and communities throughout America.

As you know, I am fully cognizant of the progress made by American Architects and Planners in their contribution to our country in contemporary design. This coupled with equal progress made in our cities by their respective governing bodies in forging ahead with vast programs of urban renewal and redevelopment leads me to comment on the manner in which these plans are actually carried out. There are throughout our land specific areas and specific buildings of historical significance or architectural excellence that are threatened by this onward march of progress. I believe that the importance of Lafayette Square lies in the fact that we were not willing to destroy our cultural and historic heritage but that we were willing to find means of preserving it while still meeting the requirements of growth in government. I hope that the same can be done in other parts of our country.

I am particularly pleased that in this case you and the architects were able to express in the new buildings the architecture of our times in a contemporary manner that harmonizes with the historic buildings.

I congratulate you on this fine start.

The Honorable Bernard L. Boutin
Administrator of General Services Administration
Washington 25, D.C.

*The important central urban space in front of the White House, the historic Lafayette Square, recently reconstructed. The symbolic value of its preservation is more profound than the details of its execution. President Kennedy's appreciation of the significance of preserving this space, harmoniously integrating the new with the old and thus preserving the basic character of the Square, saved an important link with our cultural past. Architect: John Carl Warnecke.*

*Lafayette Square, Washington, D.C. The townhouses were in danger of being razed to make way for office buildings.*

to date. Unlike the renewal of European urban centers, which almost universally follows the philosophy that historic districts and buildings of national or local significance must be preserved and enhanced, with new buildings harmoniously added, the American urban development program has not recognized to date the need for making continuity of design a primary objective of reshaping urban centers. Because of the lack of understanding that outstanding urban design cannot be produced in a vacuum, of the unwillingness to appropriate federal assistance funds for historic preservation, and of the lack of recognition of zoning historic districts in local ordinances, much of the historic urban fabric has been unnecessarily destroyed. Thus the vital and comprehensive role of historic preservation to urban design, as the dynamic of inspirational and positive urban development, has been almost totally ignored and constitutes a major weakness of urban renewal.

Before the last war American planning practices were to a large extent rather theoretically oriented because there were no adequate tools for implementation of plans. During the postwar period cities for

the first time became more interested in action programs. The inadequacy of zoning as the main tool of comprehensive planning has been recognized by planners, some of whom in recent years have been proposing official "comprehensive development regulations" as the chief arm of the comprehensive plan. An excellent exposé of the shortcomings of zoning was made by the outstanding planning philosopher John W. Reps: "Zoning is seriously ill and its physicians—the planners—are mainly to blame. We have unnecessarily prolonged the existence of a land-use control device, conceived in another era when the true and frightening complexity of urban life was barely appreciated. We have, through heroic efforts and with massive doses of legislative remedies, managed to preserve what was once a lusty infant not only past the retirement age but well into senility."[14] Zoning based on two-dimensional or inadequate planning is negative. If based on a balanced urban design plan and sound economic and fiscal policies, it can well serve as a much more positive and useful tool. Such use of zoning has to date been possible only in a handful of urban renewal areas and in planning only the most outstanding new towns.

Urban renewal controls, although in themselves far from being

[14] John W. Reps, Second Pomeroy Memorial Lecture, "Requiem for Zoning," *Planning 1964* (American Society of Planning Officials: Chicago, 1964).

*Federal architecture, characteristic of old residential areas on Capitol Hill in Washington, destroyed for a contemplated expansion of the Library of Congress.*

*Grossly confused hierarchy of values. The barbaric destruction of a great central urban space, Pennsylvania Station, dignified entrance into Manhattan, and one of the country's great transportation temples. This meaningful, integral function of the cultural life of the city is being replaced by a complex of space and structure of uncertain meaning.*

adequate to fulfill Reps' "comprehensive development regulations," have launched American urban planning into a more pragmatic and action-oriented direction. In terms of statistics alone, some 90,000 acres of land in central urban spaces will soon have been redeveloped in American urban areas. Almost 35,000 acres will be used for residential development, and this acreage is expected to generate 300,000 new, mostly privately built dwellings in central locations. Of the 1,300 urban renewal projects that had been initiated throughout the United States by 1963, only 16 percent were in cities of population of over 100,000 and almost half of the communities were with populations of less than 25,000, showing the number of smaller communities predominating. By June 1963, 129,000 structures in central urban spaces had been demolished as the result of urban renewal activities.[15] The Department of Housing and Urban Development estimated that by mid-1966 the total number of approved urban renewal projects in American communities would amount to 1,762, with an estimated 720 projects having either started or completed their redevelopment.

The broadening horizons of central urban renewal encompass the positive renewal of the physical, social, economic, cultural, political, and educational environment. In analyzing this synoptic urban renewal it is necessary to shift from a largely quantitative to a more value-oriented illustrative judgment. In the physical development of American urban hubs through urban renewal, the accomplishments in urban design furnish some examples of good architecture, and offer some solutions to the problems of private automobile parking in the centers of large metropolitan areas.

There is virtually no city in America today where there is no physical evidence of some renewal activity in its center. This in itself is

---

15 William L. Slayton, *Report on Urban Renewal.* Statement before the Subcommittee on Housing, U.S. House of Representatives, (U.S. Government Printing Office: Washington, D.C., 1963).

*Eighteenth-century gate building in the historic Society Hill section of central Philadelphia, now being rehabilitated as a residential neighborhood preserving the maximum number of structures of historic significance.*

a proof of the national scope and awareness of the problem and of some actual steps taken to save the city center. Increasingly a more positive participation on the part of the inhabitants of American communities in all aspects of urban planning has had a great civic and educational impact, resulting in a greater degree of interest and pride on the part of the urban American in his own central urban spaces. Thus the citizen of Philadelphia is becoming increasingly proud of being a Philadelphian, a phenomenon which in the past had not been connected—where it did exist—with civic pride.

As an indication of the scope of social and human problems in the renewal of central urban spaces, it can be pointed out that from the inception of the program up to 1963 over 150,000 American families had been displaced by urban renewal activities alone. In terms of figures the record of the rehousing of these families into adequate standard accommodations is quite impressive. Approximately 80 percent have been rehoused into decent, safe, and sanitary housing.[16] The Urban Renewal Administration estimated that by mid-1966 the number of families relocated as the result of urban renewal activities would have reached 215,000.

Another urban social problem on which the renewal of central urban spaces has had a significant impact is the status of American minority group families, particularly the Negroes. Of the total number of displaced families noted above, over 65 percent were Negroes. To place in perspective the effect of urban renewal upon Negro families, it is relevant to note that the Negroes constitute roughly 10 percent of the total United States population. However, because of their economic, educational, and cultural disadvantages, as well as restrictive housing practices, Negroes form the majority of urban slum dwellers.

In the economic area the stimulation of the private economy, the enlargement of tax revenues, and the increased level of employment are

[16] Ibid.

the achievements of renewal of central areas that can readily be cited. An example of the stimulation of private economy is the fact that by 1963 for the $6 billion involved in public funds, the private capital investment in the United States in central urban renewal projects amounted to $20 billion.

While stimulating the national economy considerably, urban renewal has helped cities to enlarge greatly their tax revenues, thus more than paying for itself to the municipalities. Mayor Richard Daley of Chicago has stated that the annual tax revenues from 27-odd redevelopment projects in that Midwestern city are expected to more than double. In Southwest Washington, when renewal is complete, the total tax revenues will amount to eight times the prerenewal tax revenues. Another positive economic feature of the renewal of central areas is that it is providing considerable employment opportunity in the cities.

Besides having a significant effect upon the social, economic, and physical development of the centers of American cities, renewal also has an important impact upon the educational and cultural life of central urban areas. In addition to such spectacular, but rather atypical, accomplishments as the Lincoln Center in New York City, constructed in an urban renewal area, many schools and universities have been positively affected by the process of urbanization.

# V.  THE DOLEFUL CITY: THE DILEMMA
OF CHANGING PATTERNS

## 1.  URBAN QUICKSILVER

The evolving function and character of central urban spaces as the result of transposed patterns of housing and altering modes of work, trade, and services points towards an ever-increasing form-coherence in the over-all structure of this great region. The major centers of the Northeast Megalopolis are the urban hubs of Boston, Providence, Hartford, New Haven, New York, Newark, Philadelphia, Baltimore, and Washington. The fastest growing metropolitan center of the Northeast Megalopolis is Washington, which by the year 2000 is expected to become, together with adjoining Baltimore, the "super metropolitan area," number two of this giant "city," New York being in the lead.[1]

The number one existing transportation problem of these great urban centers is moving commuters in and out of their "metro-centers" during the morning and evening rush hours, and these severe conditions are typical of the congested traffic and difficult access to these urban hubs. These drastic and grim conditions are the result of private automobile-oriented commuting and the lack of adequate modern rapid-transit systems within as well as outside the centrum. The public intracity transportation of Baltimore, which consists exclusively of buses, lost 50 percent of its transit passengers in the short span of one decade, between 1949 and 1959.[2] The bus companies, privately operated and insufficiently equipped, do not provide today a satisfactory alternative to private automobile commuting, however inadequate the latter may be

[1] In 1930 Washington ranked sixth among the centers of this region; in 1960 it ranked fourth, with New York, Philadelphia, and Boston being ahead.

[2] Baltimore Department of Transit and Traffic, *Baltimore Transit Study,* Part I (Baltimore, 1958).

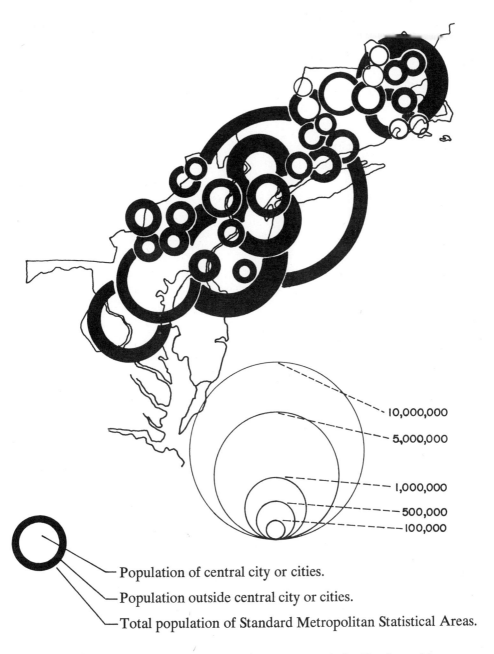

10,000,000

5,000,000

1,000,000

500,000
100,000

————Population of central city or cities.

————Population outside central city or cities.

————Total population of Standard Metropolitan Statistical Areas.

*Population of Standard Metropolitan Statistical Areas of the Northeast Meg-alopolis—1960.*

in terms of comfort, speed, or parking convenience. The changing pattern of travel within the megalopolitan centers of the postwar period is exemplified by Providence, where during a 14-year period total travel doubled, private automobile travel increased 5-fold, and mass transportation usage decreased to only one-fourth of its 1946 level.[3]

Washington's commuting problem to the downtown area is one of the worst among the inner cities of the Northeast Megalopolis for the following reasons: (1) Washington's population has been extremely automobile-conscious since the 1920's—statistics show an unusually high ratio of automobiles to population since that period—with the resulting maximum use of private automobiles and a minimum use of public transportation, (2) greater Washington is an urban sprawl, and (3) the Potomac River divides the metropolitan area. Bridges and their approaches are inadequate to cope with rush-hour traffic, and this causes great bottlenecks for the daily commuter to the heart of Washington. The intensity of traveling into and out of the inner city in the Washington area is illustrated by the fact that in 1955 over 1.6 million people entered and left the District in an average day.[4] The total regional population was then 1,870,000. The population of the national capital region is expected to reach 3.7 million by the year 1985, and the increased mobility of this population is estimated by the National Capital Planning Commission to generate 7.5 million trips per day in that year. Metropolitan Washington has, for example, far fewer suburban satellite employment centers than does New York, and thus the inner city generates more traffic per capita than does the greatest and most congested centrum of the megalopolis—Manhattan. In recent years the number of people that entered Manhattan daily is estimated at a little

[3] Providence City Plan Commission, *Downtown Providence 1970* (Providence, 1961).

[4] Joint Committee on Washington Metropolitan Problems, United States Senate, *Washington Metropolitan Area Transportation Problems* (U.S. Government Printing Office: Washington, D.C., 1958), pp. 81–110.

more than 3 million persons out of the total population of the New York metropolitan region of some 16 million people.[5] Even when compared with the larger megalopolitan center of Philadelphia, the total number of commuters entering central Washington is still astronomical, and in 1955 travel to the hub of this international center was considerably more than twice that of the movement into the inner city of Philadelphia. The predominance of white-collar employment in Washington's inner urban area is responsible for this disproportionately greater number of people traveling daily to its center.

The victory of the private-automobile mode of transportation over public transport in and out of the megalopolitan urban cores—responsible for the great congestion of inner streets and outer access routes—is visible even in communities like Boston, well known for their efficient and relatively long-established rapid-transit systems of the prewar era.

In Boston by 1956 more than half of the 560,000 persons entering the downtown area commuted by private automobile, and the railroad and mass-transit facilities continued to lose passengers.[6] Similar conditions exist in New York, where the number of motor vehicles entering the urban hub on weekdays has been constantly rising, from 382,000 in 1948 to 519,000 in 1956, while the actual number of persons entering and leaving this great urban center declined in the 1950's as the result of decentralization of employment.

Thus, the existing macabre congestion of the inner streets of the urban centers of the Northeast Megalopolis becomes constantly worse, irrespective of whether the number of people entering their centrums is slightly declining as in the case of Manhattan, is on a more-or-less stabilized basis as in the hub of Philadelphia, or is on the increase as in the case of Washington.

[5] Committee on Interstate and Foreign Commerce, United States Senate, *Commuter Transportation* (U.S. Government Printing Office: Washington, D.C., 1961), p. 3.

[6] Boston College Seminar Research Bureau, *Transportation Facts and Public Policy for Downtown Boston,* College of Business Administration (Boston, 1958).

*The graceful road ribbon from a natural setting has here been superimposed over an urban pattern, in effect creating a man-made river for high-speed travel that requires bridging. Interstate highway cutting through Pawtucket, Rhode Island and Attleboro, Massachusetts.*

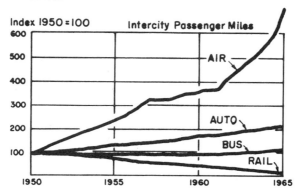

*Intercity traffic growth. Since 1950, while intercity automobile passenger miles doubled, intercity passenger miles by airplanes increased approximately sevenfold.*

The excellent interurban-center communication network of the megalopolis today, both highway and airway, provides a superb inter-connection for its rather well-integrated metropolitan regions, particularly along its major axial spine.

The changing interurban-center modes of transportation further aid and abet the existing trend towards the ultimate choking of the inner streets with "soft" vehicles. The airlines have taken over from the "hard" intercity railroad passenger transportation, capable of delivering a great number of persons into the most dense sections of the urban core, and today drop thousands of intercity commuters on the fringes of megalopolitan centers, thus necessitating their transfer to a central destination by modes of secondary and additional systems, usually "soft," consisting of taxis and limousines, to add further to the congestion of the inner streets in particular and the movement to and within the urban core in general. The main south-north axis of interurban megalopolitan travel lies between Washington and Boston, and today, in addition to regularly scheduled intercity airlines communication, there exists a shuttle-type airplane commuting service, indicating a constantly increasing trend towards interurban-center activities within the daily life of the megalopolis.

The improvement and ease of interurban transportation parallels the increase in the problems of intraurban travel, and this dichotomy is responsible for the changing functions of the individual urban centers and constant strengthening of the structure of the megalopolis. It is not uncommon today for a businessman in Boston to leave home after breakfast, spend the day in the centrum of Washington, and be back in Boston for dinner.

The great increase in the number of privately owned automobiles into and out of the central urban spaces has, besides the choking of inner-street traffic, resulted in gargantuan parking problems in the heart of the city and in taking the most valuable urban land away from human usage and donating it in its entirety to the service of the motorcar. The effect of the private automobile upon the pattern of the urban core envinces itself significantly in this problem. There is not enough land available today in urban centrums of the megalopolis to park all private automobiles entering the core. To provide this space would be uneconomical from all points of view. Even before World War II parking lots occupied tremendous areas of the American center-city; a dramatic example is downtown Los Angeles, which as far back as 1938 consisted of 50 percent in parking lots.

Today, two governmental legal tools are being employed to provide parking in central urban spaces. The first one, through the zoning ordinance, requires parking provisions, based on the building's floor area and type of occupancy, for a specified number of cars on the property of all newly constructed buildings. In downtown Washington this law has resulted in the provision for parking under new buildings, mostly through tortuous, congested entrances and exits difficult—often impossible—to access. The impact of this attempt to cope with the urban-core parking problem by the zoning ordinance alone has manifested itself in the design of these new buildings as well. In most cases of private development of the heart of the city, the lot area upon which a pro-

*Result of the victory of motor over man. Extremely valuable central urban land devoted to storage of automobiles.*

posed new building is to be constructed is either insufficient in size or shape, or both, to permit the development of underground parking facilities in adequate numbers. This means, in effect, that parking becomes the final deciding factor in determining the size and shape of the building, and architectural and urban design elements hardly enter the picture. A hypothetical example of design by parking is seen in an office building to be constructed in the downtown area on a lot 60 feet wide by 100 feet deep in an area of the city that allows a maximum of ten stories. Since one car space is required for every 600 square feet of floor space, this building, in order to obtain a building permit, must provide on the same property a minimum of 100 parking spaces. Because mechanical parking provisions cannot be justified economically, the maximum number of cars which can be accommodated, even theoretically, in a triple-deck underground garage amounts to 30. In reality only one-level parking would be feasible. This type of control is partially responsible for the hacked-up skyline of central urban areas of today and for the design of downtown structures being determined by zoning provisions rather than by urban design principles.

The second method employed today to provide a maximum of off-street parking in the urban core is found in the redevelopment areas of urban central spaces, where in many cases private developers are required to provide hundreds of parking spaces below ground in double or triple tiers to serve the new buildings above. This method, from the point of view of design alone, is more satisfactory than are the arbitrary zoning provisions, as the parking is judged an integral part of the total design from the start—but it adds to street congestion in almost the same way as does the downtown parking garage. In the densely congested urban cores of the megalopolis, provisions for additional parking spaces actually magnify the inflow of private automobiles into the center and multiply the problem. Since Washington at the present time does not have in operation a satisfactory alternate system to private auto-

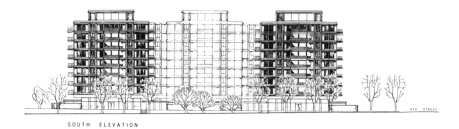

SOUTH ELEVATION

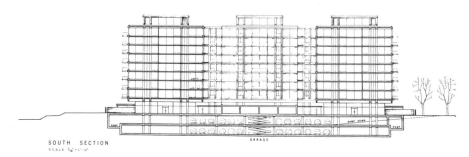

SOUTH SECTION
SCALE 1/16" = 1'-0"

*Integration of parking with apartment housing in an urban center.*

mobile transportation, these measures may be judged necessary from a short-term point of view, but as soon as an adequate public transportation system is built, these expensive facilities may well become a detriment to a development based upon a truly efficient transportation system, particularly within the urban core itself.

The urban cores of Boston and New York were among the first of the megalopolitan centers to recognize that in order to solve traffic and parking problems, public transportation systems must be improved and that to attempt to control the former while leaving the latter unattended was a hopeless exercise. Boston, earlier than any other urban center of the postwar era, recognized that something must be done to keep through-travel away from its urban core and to provide a balanced system of private and public transportation. In the early 1950's a circumferential highway was built around the city, and it proved to be such a success in diverting through-traffic from the urban core that it has since been copied by Philadelphia, Baltimore, and other communities, most recently by Washington, in building these circumventing bypasses for long-distance traffic.

Boston was also the first megalopolitan center to attempt to inaugurate a balanced transportation system by providing large parking facili-

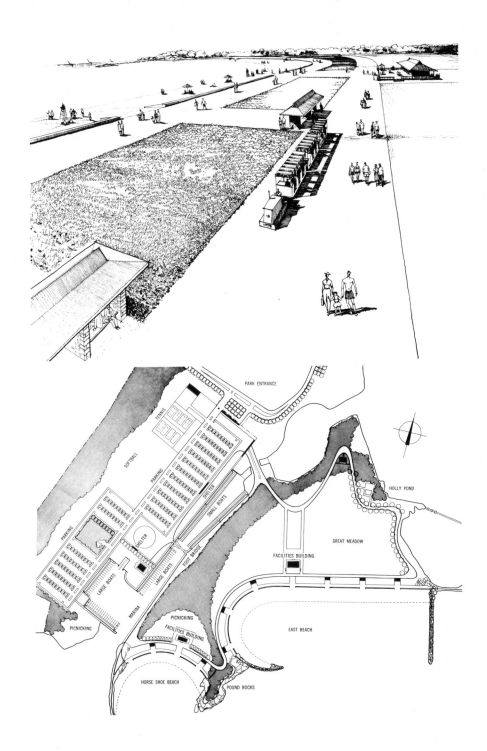

A "park-and-ride" system used in conjunction with urban recreation central space. The indigenous character of the natural land formation is accentuated by the orchestrated alignment of the road ribbon and the use of "minicars" for slow transit. Cove Island Park, Stamford, Connecticut.

An attempt to integrate interstate and intracity bus terminals with parking and a motor hotel in the center of Washington, D.C.

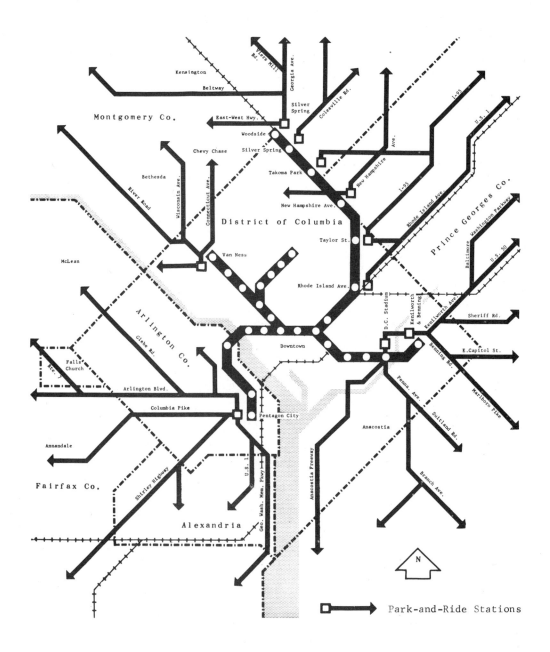

*Proposed public subway system for Washington, D.C., with private park-and-ride stations.*

ties at the terminal stations of its rapid transit system in the early 1950's and most stations along a line newly constructed in 1959. In providing convenient and comfortable "park-and-ride" facilities along its major rapid-transit lines leading to the very centrum of Boston, this megalopolitan center pioneered in attempting to solve the problem of commuting to the center-city through balanced, combined private and public, "soft" and "hard" modes of transportation.

## 2. THE CAST-OUTS

The changing modes of transportation and their significant impact upon the pattern, form, and function of central urban spaces are vividly expressed in the existing conditions of megalopolitan urban cores. Less visible and thus more subtle, yet equally important, are the basic elements of urban life—housing, employment, and services—all of which are in no less flux and undergoing no less of a fundamental change than the forms which express them: the hard core, the transitionary area, and the whole urban organism.

Residential occupancy, although taking up the great majority of land in urban areas today, constitutes the smallest land use in the hard core of central districts, which are mainly occupied by the "working" activities and functions of the city. The historical distinction between the traditional "downtown"—where people work, transact business, and congregate together—and the "uptown" where people live—is still quite discernible. However, the distinctions between the inner core and outer core do begin to show signs of functional interpenetrations as some service and employment places begin to move away from the center, and housing density builds up in the intermediate zone and even invades the core itself.

The suburban housing sprawl of the last 20 years was a natural out-

*The mediocre and boring suburban sprawl of outer metropolitan rings.*

come and a continuation of the early twentieth-century trend of a much faster rate of growth of the suburban rings than the old, hard urban core. In the first half of this century the percentage of people living in the outer metropolitan ring more than doubled, from 11 percent in 1900 to 24 percent in 1950, and this trend has continued to date.[7] The greatest housing density is contained in the intermediate ring that lies between the hard core of the city and the outer metropolitan rings.

Housing contained in the outer metropolitan rings consists mainly of postwar privately owned single-family dwellings built on an individual lot. Much of this construction is partially prefabricated and possesses the typical look-alike form that distinguishes the American suburban development of the last 20 years. The intermediate rings consist generally of older, prewar housing, mostly single dwellings, some row-housing, and two- and three-story garden-type apartments. The intermediate ring that immediately surrounds the hard urban core consists in some places of high-rise apartments ranging from luxury-type to middle-income units, both of prewar and postwar construction; but the great majority of the inner intermediate rings consist of townhouses and row-houses that are blighted, dilapidated slums. The same deplorable housing conditions generally exist in the hard core itself, although in smaller numbers.

The doleful existing housing conditions within the urban centers of America are illustrated by the fact that in 1964, 12 million of the 45 million urban dwellings in the United States were considered "substandard," inadequate, and deteriorating, and of those 12 million, 7 million were considered unfit for human habitation, beyond repair, and unsalvageable. It is this utter deterioration of housing in and around the

---

[7] Donald J. Bogue, *Population Growth in Standard Metropolitan Areas 1900–1950*, Housing and Home Finance Agency (U.S. Government Printing Office: Washington, D.C., 1953), p. 18.

urban cores of the megalopolis that has provided the opportunity for replanning and reshaping the old centers.

The socioeconomic implications of these housing conditions and their impact upon the function and form of central urban spaces of the megalopolis are far-reaching and extremely complex. The recent urban unrest and revolt spring to a large degree out of these inhuman living conditions that have been aggravated by the great postwar migration of underpriviledged and uneducated Negroes from predominantly rural areas into the inner cores of urban centers. Census figures indicate this growth of Negro population in various centers of the megalopolis over a 20-year period. Between 1940 and 1960 the percentage of the nonwhite population of New York, Philadelphia, and Washington approximately doubled, and today the population of the District of Columbia is more than 60 percent Negro. This postwar sociocultural revolution in the urban cores has further accelerated the changing function and form of the central city. The typical prewar, single-story, brick row-housing of Baltimore and Washington, which gave the intermediate outer rings their unique and indigenous character, has almost completely been taken over by underprivileged families, and in a short period of 20 years has been turned into slums.

The existing problem of housing in urban centers is basically an economic and sociopolitical one and is most intimately affected by economic limiting factors as well as by political and legal boundaries. Since until the enactment of the Housing and Urban Development Act of 1965 there existed few control measures for shaping balanced housing in central urban areas, the economics of free enterprise remains the strongest influencing force in this developmental pattern. We can witness the deteriorating slum areas occupied by low-income families, and the luxurious apartment houses and townhouses side by side in and around urban cores. In Manhattan the millionaires' row of Upper East Side and the Harlem ghetto; in Washington Georgetown and the Negro

*The elegant, urbane character of prewar residential spaces in the ring sur-rounding the work center.*

*Housing in the hard core. An example of the depressing urban environment which gave impetus to the flight to suburbia.*

districts. Similarly, other central urban areas of the megalopolis offer examples of social and economic contrasts that form a serious block towards shaping unified and balanced central urban spaces. Economic inequities have forced the great majority of middle-income families into the outer rims of urban development and outside the heart of truly urban life.

The physical form of central urban spaces is equally affected by this imbalance. One of the major problems of shaping central residential spaces is the inherent difficulty of redeveloping urban land even with government subsidies at today's high building and land costs, and then being able to reuse it for low-income housing. The great majority of slum areas in the Southwest residential center in Washington and in other urban centers have been replaced by apartments that are beyond the rental means of low-income and lower-middle-income groups.

From the urban design point of view of improving the process of shaping the central urban spaces, the lack of comprehensive, three-dimensional planning particularly manifests itself in housing design, since housing forms the great majority of land usage of urban areas. Since the majority of housing in the megalopolis consists of privately owned, owner-occupied dwellings, government controls are extremely difficult; planning implemented through zoning is spotty, haphazard, and inconclusive, and little compositional form and hierarchy of volumes can be superimposed. However, the developments in renewal activities, particularly in the field of urban residential design, show hopeful signs that the problem is being recognized and that through increased governmental assistance and attention on a large metropolitan scale, conditions will improve. The value of housing, exclusive of land, in urban centers continues to constitute nearly one-quarter of the total national wealth. The estimated value of all residential structures in urban communities in America in 1955 was 320 billion dollars. From this investment point of

view and from the magnitude of human values that it represents, housing in urban centers deserves close attention. The degree of success with which this problem will be solved will to a large extent determine the future of the megalopolis and of its central spaces.


3.  HUB DYNAMICS

Although employment and services occupy only a fraction of metropolitan land area taken up by housing, they form the very essence of urban life and functions of central urban spaces. The hard-core area of Washington, which contains no more than five square miles, provides employment for one-third of the total labor force of the Washington metropolitan area and the great majority of its brainpower. In 1960 this area employed 275,000 people, approximately half of them in government service, the remainder in private business.[8] While since the war this urban core has increased in magnitude and importance as an employment center, its function as the center of services and retail sales has continuously diminished, from containing approximately one-third of the retail sales of the metropolitan area to only approximately 15 percent today.

Similar conditions exist in the megalopolitan core of mid-Manhattan. Its central business district, an area less than eight square miles, provides employment for over 1.5 million people. More than half of these workers are employed in a three-square-mile area in the center of this hard core. The dynamic growth of this great urban centrum continues at a rapid pace, with more than 45 million square feet of new office space having been added to this already great concentration of buildings between 1947 and 1963, and with more than two-thirds of this

[8] Economic Associates, *Prospective Growth of the Washington Metropolitan Area and Its Central Core,* Vol. I (Washington, D.C., 1963).

construction centered in the upper cores of the East Side of mid-Manhattan.[9]

The transformation of the city into a megalopolitan core has been partially responsible for the present growth dynamics of these hubs as employment centers. Further analysis of this phenomenon indicates that the activities of an urban core of megalopolitan magnitude can function smoothly only if they are well supported by related services. Also the traditional goods-distribution activities as well as the central retail functions of the center have to a large degree become dispersed outside the hub and those remaining have become related in character.

The services of today's urban central area have changed from being goods-oriented to being people-oriented. Manufacturing has left the center-city except for small product industries where productivity per worker is high and requires highly skilled labor and related services. Consumer services, on the other hand, are scattered throughout the core because they are closely related to other central-core activities.

Another element of urbanization responsible for the great emphasis and growth of megalopolitan centrums as employment centers has been the white-collar revolution and automation, which require centralization. As far back as 1950 the percent of white-collar workers in the Washington metropolitan area exceeded more than half of the total labor force, and this mark was almost reached in the New York metropolitan area. This trend is rapidly increasing, intensifying the need for an ever-higher density of employment in megalopolitan cores. Since even with improved transportation the central business district will not be able to compete with neighborhood shopping centers, the future of retail sales in the core is expected to serve the secondary shoppers—people employed in the core—rather than the buyers who would come downtown for the express purpose of purchasing.

[9] Figures quoted taken from a publication by New York-New Jersey Transportation Agency, *Journey to Work* (New York, 1963).

The dynamic growth of the urban hub as the citadel of work has given rise to dramatic new construction. The axis routes bringing in hundreds of thousands of workers daily to the city express the intimate relationship of the lifelines and the hub.

Bridges around the Jefferson Memorial in the Nation's capital. Disunity of the roads and bridges is rather jarring in this horizontal space.

A poetic expression of a paved ribbon to an urban setting—ultimate harmony of structure and space. The Verrazano Narrows Bridge between New York City and Staten Island carries twelve lanes of traffic.

Land-use analysis, as well as examination by function of the central business floor space in the major urban centers of the megalopolis, gives the following summary of existing conditions: decentralization of retailing and services has caused a shrinkage of commercial land use within the central cores; office-space demand in the heart of the city shows a constant growth and occupies by far an increasing percentage of total available floor space; residential land use is infinitesimal in the hard core and uniformly amounts to the smallest function of the heart of the city.

# VI.  THE METROPOLIS OF AMERICA: GREAT EXPECTATIONS

## 1.  TERMINAL TEMPLES

Every age builds temples expressive of its cultural values and dedicated to the gods that form the central theme of a specific page of human history. Temples of today's megalopolitan culture are being built to transportation—one of the chief determinants of urban structure and an indispensable ingredient of the matrix of urban life.

The entrance to the urban core, whether by an individual or a public mode of transportation, forms the significant and lasting first impression—an introduction to the functions and forms within. Since the individual mode of transportation has, up to now, won the tug-of-war, and the automobile has successfully held back the development of efficient mass rapid-transit systems for megalopolitan areas, the major gateways to urban centers are the roads feeding the ever-increasing number of motor vehicles into the already congested core.

The majority of roads that lead into the great regional centrums are extremely poorly designed and laid out without the slightest consideration of highway esthetics. In contrast with the intercity highways, which often produce exhilarating spatial experiences through adroit and harmonious integration with the landscape, the majority of roads leading into the city are ugly and demoralizing. The lack of visible form and meaning in the entrance to the city is the result of gross insensitivity to the impact that such mediocrity has upon the people who travel daily on these roads. The depressing urban environment created by an almost total rejection of planning and design principles in constructing these freeways and roadways in high-density urban areas is further worsened by the chaotic, ugly, and disturbing highway appurtenances: the macabre juxtaposition of road signs, commercial advertising, and utility wires

*A major entrance into the "Metropolis of America." An example of design negativism and failure to develop an historic urban space. The banks of the Potomac 200 years later.*

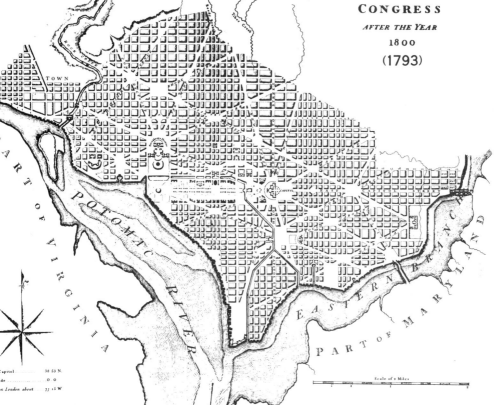

strung out in all directions. Instead of providing an encore of interest and drama expected of an approach to a great cultural center, such a view from the road repulses in the strongest of terms. What could have been a spiritually animating experience becomes a degrading trip downtown.

The vision of Washington as the "Metropolis of America" at the turn of the eighteenth century is only today materializing. Great expecta-

*Lack of design controls and of a hierarchy of values, underdevelopment of urban land. The entrance to the city and the location of service facilities express a total confusion of purpose and intent. Man's failure to control and integrate his environment.*

*Ill-functioning design. Lack of clear definition of lanes through change of texture and materials, failure to provide a sense of direction through visual artistic means, reflected by badly designed and poorly located traffic signs. Dynamics of speed and a sense of an emerging urban environment are missing. Capital Beltway.*

tions over the decades are in the mid-1960's taking form within the fastest-growing urban center on this continent. The most dramatic and visible expression of this dynamic maturing process is seen in the frantic and often controversial construction of buildings, highways, and bridges. The typical ugly urban roadway that leads into the heart of the megalopolitan core can be found in ample array in this metropolitan area. However, the central urban spaces of this great district also contain some of the best examples of parkway design to be found anywhere. Some of these follow the original pattern of open spaces and landscaped areas of L'Enfant's great plan, among which the Rock Creek Parkway provides a superb example of an indigenous wedge of topography winding through dense urban areas and terminating in its monumental core. From this Maryland gateway the sculpture of the city's skyline, the graceful, soaring overpasses, and the eurhythmic mastery of alignment and man-made panorama are all-pervasive. Equally masterfully conceived are some of the significant approaches from Virginia, among which the George Washington Memorial Parkway is a classic example. Intimately hugging the palisades, its design courageously discards any trace of acknowledgment of petty and insignificant land forms. The inherent strength of the entire length of this great artifact lies in the confident, yet respectful and dignified, use of natural forms, to provide a truly inspiring series of processional experiences in approaching the center of the Metropolis of America.

Both the creatively conceived and the uninspired ugly highways leading to the great urban centers have one common negative feature: they funnel more and more vehicles into the already erupting core. For Washington, divided by a body of water, this also means a problem of bridging and the design of these structures. The latest act in attempting to pave the Potomac River is the Theodore Roosevelt Bridge, opened in mid-1964. This structure is the ultimate attempt of federal highway engineers to design a bridge with multiple accesses and ramps for moving

*Ultimate artistry of the highway as a gateway to the city—The George Washington Memorial Parkway approaching Washington from Virginia.*

*The confused interpenetration of space and structure—neither a bridge, nor a high-
way, nor a piece of sculpture. Theodore Roosevelt Bridge*

the maximum number of automobiles at any one time. These limpid
ramps form a mass of tentacles at each end of the bridge, occupy disproportionately vast areas of valuable urban land, split one urban space
from another, make pedestrian movement a virtual impossibility, cut
great wounds into the government and cultural central urban spaces,
and actually create traffic bottlenecks.

The purpose and intent of the designers of the Memorial Bridge,
as an expression of a dignified, strong, and welcoming gateway reflective
of the time in which it was built, does not find an equivalent meaning in
the Theodore Roosevelt structure. The dynamics of today's urban life are
only expressed in crude and insignificant forms, and this bridge is a
testimony only to the failure to provide new solutions to transportation
problems.

Even within these limitations the opportunity of truly sculpting a
significant form was lost in the Theodore Roosevelt Bridge, and the result
is a badly articulated, disjointed structure that, instead of bridging and
connecting the vital central spaces, forms yet another disturbing chasm.
The great natural landmarks and characteristic skyline are ignored.

As the dynamics of intramegalopolitan travel place a greater and
greater emphasis upon public and mass transit, adequate facilities for all
public transportation systems must be developed as an integral part of
the central urban complex. Since the decline of railroad passenger travel,
intercity long-distance buses have become the chief public ground-trans-
portation system. New York City was one of the earliest cities to recognize the need for the formulation of a powerful transportation authority
for the development of large-scale terminals. In Philadelphia the recognition that central-terminal transportation facilities form the essence of
the urban core also came early in the Market Street transportation complex. Washington has been retarded in recognizing the need for developing a well-integrated terminal center in the heart of its core. The first
impression of central urban spaces of the nation's capital at either

*Terminal facilities of a major mode of megalopolitan travel.*

of the two major intercity bus terminals belies the very character of this great urban center. These terminals, if one can apply this term to these insignificant gas stations, are located in a blighted area and themselves create and augment the blight. The foreign visitor who arrives at the gates of Washington full of awe of our technological accomplishments is stunned by the permeating feeling of soullessness of this central urban space in a world capital.

The establishment in the center of Washington of a well-designed terminal facility for all ground-type megalopolitan modes of transportation is an absolute necessity not only for the development of this metropolitan area but also for the cultural and economic growth of the entire Northeast urbanized region.

The lack of appreciation of the inherent potential of a rapid intra-megalopolitan bus transportation system, as evinced in the shortage of public and government support for its development, is expressed in its mundane and grossly inadequate central facilities. This is in sharp contrast to the enthusiasm that welcomed the railroads into the center-city in the past.

The railroad stations in the smallest urban centers, as well as in the great cities, became the focal point of the community—the place where people met, that provided a very real contact with other urban centers. This important cultural function was expressed in the design of these monuments to transportation, almost always in a direct but sophisticated manner. The Grand Central Station in New York City and the Union Station in Washington are excellent examples of the significant contributions in the exploration of the purpose and intent of central urban transportation facilities as expressed in the experimentations of plasticity and continuity of space by their designers.

These innovations and great ideas are to be found, not in the "beautification" of this temple of transportation through application of classical forms and details, but in the highly imaginative use of structure and

*Daniel H. Burnham, the great synoptic desginer, was creator of this magnificent space. Union Station, Washington, D.C.*

*"Make no little plans; they have no magic to stir men's blood. . . ."*

*From a less turbulent era, the classic elegance of this entry into the Nation's capital commands respect.*

space and their interrelationship in solving a new, exciting, and challenging problem. By discovering the inherent truth of this mode of transportation and by exaggerating it, what might have been merely a shelter for people and trains became, in the hands of creative architects, masterpieces of spatial experience.

The Union Station provides one of the most exhilarating of such experiences. Arriving by train, the visitor approaches the heart of the city through a highly articulated movement in space. The vigorous and voluminous terminal hall provides a respite after a series of rhythmical spatial experiences enjoyed while decelerating through the dense urban areas and enhances a prelude to the excitement of the federal city. The whelm of energy and the sense of drama which this urban space affords is further heightened by emerging into the transitionary space under the eurhythmic arcade, which at once offers glimpses of the identifying landmarks of this metropolis.

Although relatively little used at present, these magnificent railroad stations not only provide a profound cultural and historical continuity which must be preserved and used but also offer inspiration to the form-givers of the future. This breath of life is generally missing from the majority of air terminals, which are usually designed as material, sordid,

*The ethereal space of another great temple of transportation. Main Concourse, Grand Central Terminal, New York City.*

and poorly functioning entities. The inherent drama and excitement of air travel and the potentiality of expressing it in modern vocabulary were generally not capitalized upon by timid and mediocre designers. The result is that at best the great air terminals of the megalopolises are an uncoordinated exhibition of individual designers' skills in the use of synthetic materials—the Kennedy Airport in New York City—or at their most mediocre are no more than "hangars" for passengers, luggage, and equipment. Upon arriving at the National Airport in Washington, one is immediately distracted by the confusion, chaos, and lack of purpose and intent of this space. Unlike the magnificent views offered when approaching this urban center from the air, once on the ground the passenger as man is ignored. The opportunity of enriching his mind and soul with a meaningful diapason of harmony is lost as he is at once disappointed and disenchanted. The sensitive and individual mark of artistic accomplishment—the transformation of an inorganic material into a work of art—is missing here. These airport terminals offer little beyond a view of a boring mass of automobiles as the first impression of the cultural life of their urban centers!

The regional ramifications in planning transportation networks and their centers have so far been largely ignored, and their potential effects upon the life of the megalopolis unappreciated. The creation of a transportation planning agency for entire regional entities—responsible for planning, coordinating, and developing a balanced system of air, ground, and below-ground modes of transportation—is necessary for judicial and creative determination of the location and design of the important terminal junctions in all urban centers.

The Dulles International Airport in the Washington metropolitan area is an example of an outstanding central terminal facility in the Northeast. Its location was chosen by largely ignoring the emerging megalopolitan pattern. Although the planners responsible for this artifact made a significant contribution in applying methods of creative

*The great air temple. Dulles International Airport Terminal—by the architect virtuoso Eero Saarinen. The instruments of architecture—space and structure—used here to create a universal space indigenous of temples.*

experimentation by opening up even more expressive avenues of space, the failures of designing within a regional vacuum are equally apparent.

The distinct separation from the urban hub and the metropolitan area that this great airport serves forms its greatest weakness. The lack of an intimate and rapid connection with the center is a serious detriment to this otherwise significant space. This true temple to air transportation was designed through an intricate planning process by the great architect Eero Saarinen. The planners conducted a world-wide survey of the pattern of operations of large air terminals, studied the effects of these spaces on the traveler, examined problems involved in transfer operations, and arrived at the purpose and intent of this complex in a vigorous and highly creative manner. This purpose and intent—the design—was then transformed into a most meaningful structure and space.

This transportation complex has highly distinguishable elements. The basic features are extremely simple: a large, central, enclosed space with a dominant form, a vertical control tower, a pattern of run-ways, landscaped approaches, and parking platforms. These few elements are used to form a unique space and to define and control this oasis within the presently natural landscape. The homogeneous quality of this space is unmistakable. This center outside a center, the gate to Washington, divorced from and separated by Virginia's rolling country-side, today provides a refuge from frenetic urban tensions.

It is, however, more successful as a point of departure than a place of arrival and the entrance gate to the federal city. From the lower levels of the massive podium the intimately scaled openings in the base of the temple and the interior spaces act strongly upon the curiosity of the urbanite, inviting him to enter. Upstairs, the simplicity of the enormous interior is at once apparent as the eye becomes accustomed to the now magnetic natural light that enters between the eurhythmic and elegant structural supports, creating a magnificent space. The feeling of this great volume, with lights streaming through the large expanse of glass, creates a truly awe-inspiring universal space—indigenous of temples.

## 2. THE OPERATIVE URBAN PLACES

"Going out of business" is a familiar sign of the postwar period that has been recurring throughout American urban hubs to signify the changing function of the urban core. The surburban sprawl, which can be described as the Los Angelesization of the megalopolis, has gradually sucked out the vitality, life, and attraction potential from many commercial central urban spaces. The movement of much commercial life out of the heart of the city and into the outlying areas, accompanying the trek of housing with necessary services, has further been accelerated by the difficult access to the downtown, lack of parking, congested streets, and an often vulgar central urban environment. The inability

of urban centers to meet the changing demands and to provide for new commercial functions of the core dramatically evinces itself in the failure to provide adequate circulation and transportation in and out of as well as within the central spaces.

The plight of the downtown mercantile establishment, the unsuccessful attempts to fight the postwar trends of urbanization, and the unwillingness to recognize the new role of the centrum resulted in turning valuable central urban land into a huge ground-level, above-ground, and subterranean garage. This in turn not only failed to slow down the cancerous blight or to turn the tide but actually has accelerated the process of obsolescence in turning the downtown commercial areas into automobile ghettos.

*The nerve-jangling commercial spaces of the degenerated centrum.*

Walking through many central business spaces of the megalopolis is a grim and depressing experience, not devoid of sardonic humor. The freedom to create absolute urban chaos and the absence of a permeating over-all compositional thought have created intolerably discordant notes. Nowhere but downtown can one find a more glaring example of the results of the absolutely uncontrolled process of self-shaping of central urban spaces—the total lack of planning and urban design, lack of taste and urban propriety, in the true spirit of the urban jungle. Any sign, any color, any design is permitted, creating bizarre, nerve-jangling spaces from which the natural human reaction is to turn one's back and run away.

The problems of reshaping central business spaces in such utter chaos and disorder are awesome and point out the need for comprehensive planning and strong design controls. The tool of urban renewal, as presently employed in the process of rejuvenating these areas, has not as yet been fully developed, and will not be until it becomes truly a means of achieving comprehensive regional development and until it places a greater emphasis on urban design principles and controls. The difficult problems of transportation, land, air and underground rights, within a balanced, multidimensional design, require fresh and more comprehensive approaches and greater commitments of human resources and talents. Present methods of dealing with the forces that shape central commercial spaces have been token, trivial, and grossly inadequate.

These token measures can be seen in the attempts on the part of urban centers to solve traffic and circulation problems by substituting small and easily movable "minibuses" for regular buses, closing a few streets to traffic, introducing one-way streets, or providing municipal parking facilities. However, until the central urban spaces are shaped through synoptic design and are dependent on a convenient and efficient mass rapid transit, and until adequate controlling measures are introduced

*Recent design for the redevelopment of F Street, by Downtown Progress, a nonprofit corporation formed and financed by Washington, D.C., business and civic leaders to prepare plans for the revitalization of Downtown Washington. Architect: Chlothiel Woodward Smith.*

that will shape the spaces logically and consistently, the commercial urban center will remain a blotch upon urban culture.

In order to achieve comprehensive and imaginative urban development, creative forces of both government and business must be employed. In the redevelopment of central commercial areas, where such joint action was not present, the results are rather unfortunate and insignificant. Among more recent examples of private redevelopment of a central urban space is the business district of Rosslyn in Arlington, Virginia.

*The redevelopment of Rosslyn, Virginia. A blighted commercial area transformed into a major metropolitan employment center. The lack of over-all compositional thought and controls in the reshaping of this area has turned small-scale chaos into large-scale spatial disorder.*

This central area of Metropolitan Washington was reshaped in accordance with the design philosophy of the 1920's, thus contributing little to solving commercial problems of the 1960's. Missing the basic ingredients of comprehensiveness and the unifying quality of American life today, and rejecting the need for a central compositional thought, the result is both disunified and chaotic. One of the basic goals of redevelopment—the replacement of economically obsolescent buildings and re-use of land to "full" economic potential—was not realized. The reshaping of Rosslyn is a failure, not so much because it is ugly, but because the land was not developed to its ultimate economic potential and because it is unintegrated with the rest of the urban fabric. Surrounded by highways, it forms an isolated, chaotic island—an antisocial type of urban development, hard to get to and divorced from the city. Good urban design is good economics. It has little basically to do with whether an individual building is pleasing or not. Design in these terms can either be maximal or even less than minimal—negative.

The spatial form of Washington, D.C.—an excellent example of a horizontal urban entity—has to a large extent been determined by its predominant function as a great government center. Washington from the very beginning was conceived and designed as a capital city—The Metropolis of America—an urban center for nationwide and international activities. The Capitol building, with its dominating dome, became one of the chief determinants and limitants of this urban center's vertical height. In 1899 the maximum building height for Washington was established at 130 feet, thus preventing any structure from exceeding in height the chief symbols of this government urban center—the principal federal monuments.

The original plan for the nation's capital, adroitly laid out by Major Pierre Charles L'Enfant and George Washington in 1791, covers an area of approximately 11½ square miles. The design principles of L'Enfant were basically monumental, and the plan specifically de-

*Monotonous and mundane government office buildings in the Nation's capital.*

termined the location of the significant central urban spaces—"special places"—the circles and squares along the diagonal avenues. The transition of this monumental government city into an animated nuclear center of the new megalopolis is clearly visible in the transformation of the physical form of this great metropolis. The architecture of federal buildings until the postwar period followed a stereotyped, neoclassic, rather emasculated style. The dynamics of postwar growth of government activities and the need for new, functional office space in great

*In the past such structures often reflected an inadequate utilization of the country's design talent.*

quantities, ended this established trend. However, the lack of a comprehensive urban-design plan and of adequate architectural controls soon became visible in the uncoordinated, sporadic, and generally characterless design of postwar federal and commercial architecture.

The new public structures, timidly and mundanely designed, were located without much visible concern for the evolving nature of the new Washington. Therefore, the changing function and form of this great government center is more dynamically expressed in the sheer bulk and

*Headquarters of the Department of Housing and Urban Development, de-
signed by Marcel Breuer. This building reflects the radically improved design
policy and greater national interest in federal architecture. Its environs, by
contrast, show the lack of an over-all spatial composition. Each of the constituent federal agencies is still treated as an individual entity, an approach
which conflicts with the need for a greater amalgamation of functions and
of spaces in the urban core. Since the controls could be available, there is an
opportunity for placing emphasis on the juxtaposition of open spaces—plazas,
courtyards, communal and educational areas. This approach to a multi-block
section of the city would develop the central spaces rather than destroy them
through lack of organization and through the oppressively massive scale of
individual buildings.*

size of these office buildings than in their intrinsic architectural qualities. Because of a lack of a synoptic approach and adequate controls, federal and private office buildings during the last two decades have been placed throughout the hard urban core and its environs without much thought to the effect these operative concentrations will have upon total metropolitan development.

Owing greatly to the brilliance of the original plan concept, in which open spaces were emphasized in truly baroque tradition, the image of the central urban spaces of Washington as "white buildings in a green park" has loyally been preserved and forms its unique and most positive and promising characteristic. Therefore, it is not surprising that in the realm of the treatment of open spaces rather than in its architecture can be found Washington's contributions to the developing form of megalopolitan urban centers. Intimate and pleasant courtyards, pools, parklets, arcades, circles and squares, open vistas and well-scaled sheltered "special places"—all are becoming increasingly the all-important design elements within megalopolitan densities. It is these spaces that form the dynamic meeting ground between working functions and the other central activities and become the nucleii of the modern operative

*An example of intimate, human-scale central space. Cities need more of these tolerant urban oases.*

*The static recreational space symbolic of a less dynamic urban environment. Elegant use of architecture and landscape architecture of another era to harness space—the most intricate and evasive of all elements. Meridian Hill Park, Washington, D.C.*

urban center. There still remains in Washington a significant number of government central spaces that will soon become subject to renewal activities and will provide additional opportunity for shaping well-integrated, dynamic urban spaces.

New modes of transportation, decentralization of production, automation, and the white-collar revolution have affected all the older industrial urban centers—even those, such as Washington, whose main industry has always been government rather than business. One of the old industrial areas of Washington is located on the Potomac River, in the very heart of the city. The decline of water and rail transportation as the chief mover of industrial goods has turned this prime central urban area into blight and decay. Unfortunately, the potential of the waterfront was destroyed by constructing an ugly elevated freeway above the warehouses and factories. This area, which separates the desirable Georgetown residential urban center from the river, is also one of the main entrances into the centrum of Washington. The first and memorable impression in coming to this great city from this direction is one of revulsion, accentuated by smog and smells produced by the factories below. To date there are no definite, approved plans for reshaping this central land, although planning studies are actively continuing.

The postwar growth in government functions and related industrial research activities has brought new types of urban centers to the area. They range from the research headquarters of industrial concerns to the headquarters of private companies engaged in cybernetics, health, insurance, and education. This new type of industry, employing highly skilled white-collar workers, and with a high percentage of scientists and engineers, has further accelerated the development of this urban center into a dynamic employment center. The relationship between these industrial research activities and those of the federal government has been largely responsible for the changing function of the central urban spaces of this megalopolitan hub. It has also been a determinant of the

*The construction of the elevated freeway placed a solidifying mark on an obsolescent waterfront, thus impeding its development. This area, if redeveloped to its full potential, can become once again a truly significant urban space. Whitehurst Freeway, Washington, D.C.*

*Slums and monuments have existed side by side through the centuries of the city's history. A classic photo of urban blotch, now removed.*

movement toward a total integration of function within the core and in shaping its spaces along more sophisticated and urbane lines.

Since the representative quality of this new type of industry is important, these new spaces sometimes possess a distinguishing character. Amenities in the form of parklets or stonescape are provided, indicating a new and refreshing community design consciousness on the part of industry. During the postwar years American industry has become one of the chief patrons of the arts, and this trend holds a major promise for the cultural renaissance of central urban spaces.

The industrial spaces of the major hubs of the megalopolis may become synonymous with centers of research, of learning, and of culture, and indicate a general trend towards an ever-increasing amalgamation of all functions of urban life. The employment center, rather than the prewar commercial center, has already become the chief function of the hard urban core.

### 3.   SLUMS AND MONUMENTS

The city through history has always contained great architectural monuments—the temples, the palaces, the great cathedrals—as well as monumental spaces—the agoras, the forums, the great squares, the malls. It has also contained obsolete, deteriorating structures, predominantly housing. Urban-blight remedial measures were high at times of great periods of civilization, paralleling the construction of great spaces and great monuments. At times when this balance was upset, it almost always signaled the decline of culture.

Today we are engaged in one of the greatest building and rebuilding activities ever undertaken by man. The construction of new highways, new towns, and new bridges is accompanied by new efforts to reshape the urban core. It is too early to tell with certainty which of the paths we

*Existing residential blight. Today we are experiencing an unparalleled national interest in mass housing.*

are presently following: whether we are building individual monuments at the expense of ameliorating social and economic inequities, or whether we are attempting to provide the ideal of a safe, decent, and sanitary home for every American family at the expense of building truly inspiring and significant urban oases.

The building activities in Washington, as well as the controversies which evolve around the goals and intent of urban planning and design, comprise a real search for answers to these questions that all major urban centers of the megalopolis today face. In residential slum clearance and development, experimentation and soul-searching are particularly evident, and involve the total gamut of social, economic, political, administrative, legal, and architectural worlds. Since a great majority of housing in the urban cores of the megalopolis consist of slums, the experimentation in any city will have far-reaching implications not only

*Poorly coordinated, unharmonious relationship of housing to highway in a newly redeveloped area.*

*A skillful experiment with urban housing. It captures the intimate scale of the nineteenth-century townhouse expressed in new form and new materials. Architect: Charles Goodman.*

*In-town living organized around a carefully landscaped court.*

Architect: I.M. PEI

188  LAND OF URBAN PROMISE

*Monumental urban space expressive of a mutual exchange between man, space, and structure. The rhythmical organization of landmarks across space and of their statodynamic proportions creates a subduing and enthralling mood. Lincoln Memorial, Washington, D.C.*

*In the hands of creative designers, trees become structural elements which define, articulate, and enhance space. With increased building densities in urban centers the tree-lined avenue and urban orchard take on a special significance.*

*A truly tolerant urban oasis, with water the center of attraction. Rawlins Park, Washington, D.C.*

*"Reciprocity of view" created through a skillful juxtaposition of art and nature by the great synoptic designer George Washington and recognized through elegant and sensitive restoration and preservation.*

upon future residential redevelopment of the rest of that city but also upon the shaping of other centers.

The experimentation with urban housing and the attempt to find new solutions to residential urban redevelopment are exemplified in the Southwest Redevelopment Area. This central urban space, formerly occupied by the city's worst slums, has been completely cleared and rebuilt, and now contains varying housing solutions by a number of outstanding architects. The problems encountered in reshaping this area typify those encountered by other cities: total clearance, token and insignificant attention to cultural and historical continuity, lack of an overall predominating compositional thought, planning in a metropolitan and regional vacuum, insufficient attention to the original occupants of the land, and generally the lack of a guiding philosophy of purpose and intent. These unresolved dilemmas express themselves only too well in the evolved form of the architecture of this residential complex.

Washington is unique among the centers of the megalopolis in being well endowed with cultural and historical structures, but what distinguishes this capital from other capitals of the world are the great cultural open spaces that have so magnificently been designed and preserved for recreational purposes. The word "recreate" means to refresh or to entertain. Thus, in the true sense of this word urban recreation can be viewed as an extremely broad and all-inclusive concept—any urban experience that man finds refreshing and entertaining. Urban recreation means the degree of success of urban design in the creation of a truly significant, refreshing urban environment. L'Enfant's refined design clearly indicated his desire to create the greatest possible number of refreshing and entertaining views, vistas, and panoramas, and a variety of experiences as one moved along the wide avenues created, in his own words, for "reciprocity of view."

The mall, the central element of the design plan, was envisioned by L'Enfant as a grand promenade lined on both sides with embassies of

*Spontaneous and undesigned urban space indigenous of historical waterfronts of Eastern cities.*

foreign nations—the central plan of the city, the site of grand entertainment, great parades—all wonderfully refreshing. The unusable green and rather dead lawn that this space has become in subsequent years is in direct contrast to the designer's original concept.

Equally significant in this design was the conscious lack of zoning and conscious integration of the various functions and forms of the town. L'Enfant hesitated not to integrate the townhouse with the market place and the water transportation center with a government building. To L'Enfant the very essence of urban life was the variety of activities going on in the center. This to him was true urban recreation.

# VII.  URBAN REAPPRAISAL: SHAPING THE EMERGING CONURBATION

## 1.  THE MEGALOPOLITAN TRAVELER

The Northeast Megalopolis may in the future serve as a model for emerging conurbations. The experimentations, the failures, and the successes in solving its problems now and in the future will be closely watched by other supermetropolitan regions.

Since transportation is the most important inherent vital force of regional development, it has a significant and ever-increasing impact upon urban and regional planning theories and upon the changing forms of central urban spaces in particular. A well-coordinated transportation system designed to serve the newly established regional pattern of the megalopolis and the concentrated traffic volumes in and around the urban cores will determine the degree of success of land use, of the use of people's time, and of the functions of these urban hubs.

The task of providing over-all interurban center and subcenter transportation, totally integrated with the intercity and intraurban-core transportation systems, to move the greatest numbers of people with maximum comfort in and out of these urban hubs during peak-hour traffic, is one of the top-priority problems facing the megalopolitan planner. The need for high-density transfer points of the various modes of transportation, located in major and minor centers, will particularly affect the shaping of central urban spaces.

Developments in interurban-center air travel have advanced further than other modes of megalopolitan transportation. However, the increase of speed provided by intramegalopolitan jet travel is more than offset by delays caused by air congestion around airports and airport-to-center-city travel time. The use of helicopters for transportation between airport and urban core, and for other urban trips, has also proven of limited

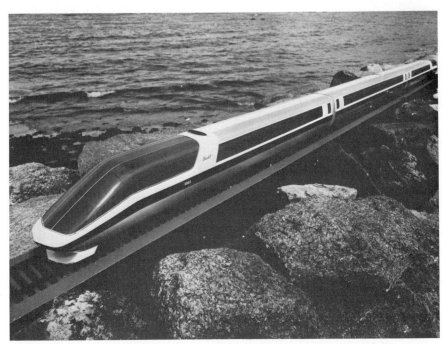

*The Budd Company's 160-mile-per-hour proposed superspeed train.*

*St. Louis Car Division of General Steel Industries' concept for a conventionally powered train capable of speeds up to 150 miles per hour. Designer: Carl W. Sundberg.*

*The rapid improvement of rail transportation of the spine of the Northeast Mega-lopolis, the Boston-New York-Washington corridor, has been recognized as being of vital importance to the development of urban centers and to the orderly growth of the entire region. Significant increases in speed, comfort, and convenience are necessary before intracity rapid-rail service can offer a real alternative to air travel and expressways.*

assistance in fast and efficient transfer of passengers. Even with the construction of efficient center transfer points to subway, rail, and other systems, it appears that the maximum future use of high-speed air transport will be in the realm of intercontinental and intracontinental urban-center travel.

The revival of interurban-center mass rapid transit on rails seems to be destined for the greatest emphasis and development in the future and to provide the greatest hope for solving the problems of intra-megalopolitan transportation. Air-cushion train designs have been developed that would employ a 15- to 30-thousandth–inch cushion of air; these wheelless vehicles operating on rails would travel at speeds in excess of 200 miles per hour, powered by means of jets and braked by reverse thrust and mechanical gripping of the rails. A number of megalopolitan railroads have already shown interest in air-supported trains.

Greater speed and more comfort in interurban-center rail travel is expected to more than double the potential capability of railroads to deliver passengers to the heart of the megalopolitan core from distances ranging from 200 to 600 miles. The transfer of these passengers onto the streets and into the intracity and intraurban-core transportation systems poses challenging urban design problems.

One of the more recent concepts that attempt to translate this multi-system interchange into a definite urban-design form is the Philadelphia City Planning Commission's scheme for the central station in downtown Philadelphia, which proposes to combine all transportation systems into a single, integrated central transportation terminal in the heart of this great megalopolitan center. Among the various types of transportation provided for within this complex is a 3,000-car above-ground parking garage. The terminal for all local and long-distance buses is to be placed directly below the garage in this proposed design, which intends to make a clear separation between road transportation facilities (buses and autos), placed at above-ground levels, and rail transportation (railroad

*A pneumatic train was constructed under Broadway in New York City almost a hundred years ago. Today's most revolutionary answer to the need for superspeed mass transit in megalopolitan areas is based upon similar principles.*

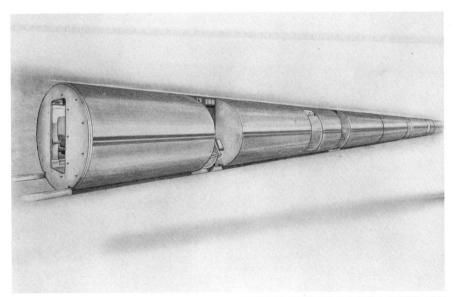

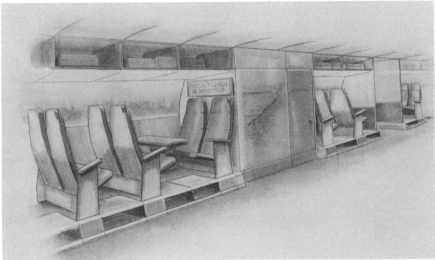

*The high-speed tube transportation placed in an underground tunnel of the 400-odd miles between Boston and Washington would cut the travel distance between these two great centers of the Northeast region to a comfortable 90 minutes, moving 4,500 passengers in a single hour. Being concealed completely underground, it could become well integrated into dense urban areas, eliminate noise and air pollution, and, most important, reduce surface congestion. Tube Transit, Inc.*

*Port Authority of Alleghany County Rapid Transit Demonstration Project— the fully automated, rubber-tired Westinghouse Transit Expressway. This private right-of-way system is particularly well adapted to metropolitan areas of medium population density. Among its chief advantages are its luxurious riding quality, smooth starts and stops, flexibility to meet rush-hour as well as off-peak-hour requirements, economy of construction, and reasonable operating costs. Each roadway consists of two concrete tracks, a central guide beam, and distribution rails. The lightweight vehicles run on four pairs of dual rubber tires and are guided by horizontally placed rubber tires that firmly secure the vehicle to the roadway.*

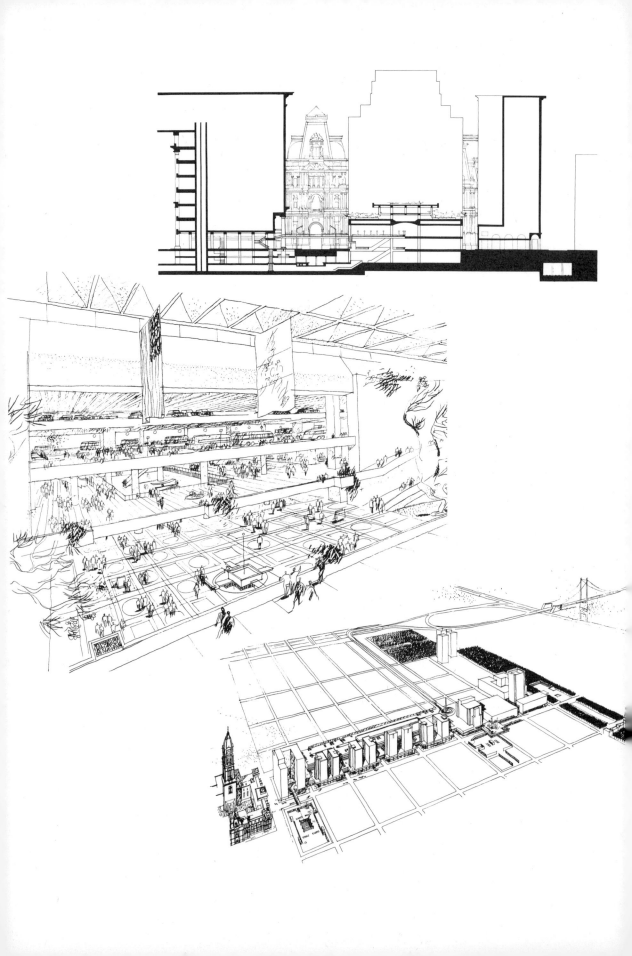

*Philadelphia City Planning Commission's Market East Study, 1963.*

*A more recent proposal for the development of the same area—1964 Study.*

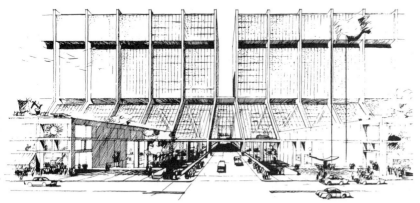

*Market East Study, interior perspective.*

*Market East Study, longitudinal section.*

and rail rapid transit), located underground. The pedestrian circulation system would be totally integrated into this design, with people freely moving about underneath the streets, divorced from street traffic and from the motorcar.

Internal transportation within this great center would hinge on the electric trolley spinal line, which would run the full length of the pedestrian mall. The moving sidewalk system would collect people from the underground railroad station, the subway, the bus terminal, and the parking garage and distribute them on the elevated promenade connecting all major department stores. The design of this extensive multilevel center deserves attention as a pioneering effort attempting to integrally combine employment, services, and transportation in a megalopolitan hub.

Individual-owned modes of transportation in one form or another will remain as the basic element of intramegalopolitan movement and will decrease only in the area in which the private automobile has already proved most ineffective, that is, intraurban-core and house-to-urban-core travel. Among new concepts of five alternative transportation systems investigated for Philadelphia by the Penn-Jersey Transportation Study is a wholly automated network of arterial highways. The basic assumption behind the automated control of private and public automobiles, trucks, and buses is that automation will double the average speed on freeways, increase greatly the safety factor, and by increasing the capacity potential will make fewer lanes necessary than on conventional highways. Because of the greatly increased volume of vehicles which could be delivered safely and efficiently to terminal locations, automated urban highways in megalopolitan centers would only multiply the already gargantuan parking problems that exist in urban cores. However, the partial automation of intramegalopolitan interstate highway systems is urgently needed to increase the safety and the carrying capacity of this highway network.

*The attempt to direct congested traffic in urban areas through remote control is yet another indication that the automobile in its present form has outlived its usefulness as an intraurban-center mode of transportation. Monitoring and control center viewing fourteen locations and controlling speeds on the John Lodge Freeway in Detroit.*

*The development of efficient intracity modes of transport is vital to meaningful reshaping of urban centers. Of the many presently tested, fully automated systems specifically developed for intracity travel, one of the most adaptable to dense urban conditions is the Teletrans System. It consists of individual electronically operated vehicles that travel through small tubes and are powered by electromagnetic drive, while the entire system is computer controlled. At the recommended speed in urban areas of 45 m.p.h., this system can move 9,000 cars per hour in a single line. The versatility and flexibility of this system are its outstanding assets. Not only the system itself but the design and location of the stations should be totally integrated with the microenvironment.*

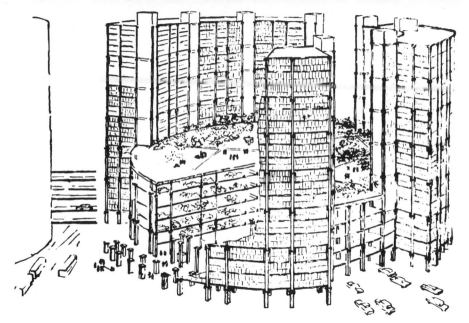

*In search of form: harbors and gateways for Philadelphia designed by Louis Kahn.*

The parking of the private automobile in and around the hard core of central urban spaces has taxed the imagination of American urban planners and architects. Proposals include such provocative schemes as Louis Kahn's huge circular parking structures containing parking provisions as integral parts of central urban functions and designed to encircle the Philadelphia downtown area—that great American architect's highly imaginative forms expressed as symbolic gates to the heart of the innercity. Among creatively designed garage structures actually constructed, an outstanding example is Paul Rudolph's garage built in downtown New Haven. Designed by one of America's foremost architects, this gutty, masculine garage structure expresses a certain excitement derived from its form and function. Yet, however architecturally interesting, this structure contributes little to the urban design of central New Haven.

An interesting new concept for underground mechanical parking of private automobiles, intimately integrated with a new high-density center-city development, is a scheme proposed for downtown Dallas by Columbia University students and faculty of planning and architecture. Recognizing and accepting the limited usefulness of the private automobile in the core of the city, this scheme is consciously based on the assumption that the preservation of subterranean and above-ground floor

*Main Place, Dallas, Texas, is the story of private redevelopment of an urban center through youthful enthusiasm, courage, and vision. The redevelopment plans proposed in 1962 by Columbia University students of architecture and planning for a 10-acre site in the center of the city have served as an impetus for present reshaping of the area.*

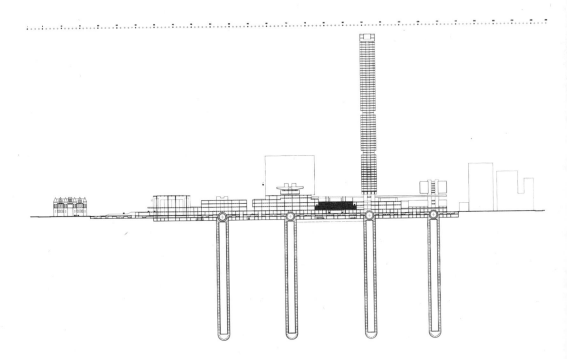

space is more valuable for purposes other than storage of cars and that this preservation is more important than the speed with which a car can be retrieved from its berth. Storage space of automobiles consists, in this concept, of a series of vertical pits, over 600 feet deep, containing a mechanically revolving conveyor capable of storing 680 cars. The system is designed to work as follows: passenger places motor car on a slowly moving horizontal conveyor (ten feet per minute) towards the continuously moving (46 feet per minute) vertical conveyor. According to the designers, under fully loaded conditions, each of the four horizontal conveyors in each pit can impact and eject an automobile every 22 seconds; thus the motorist can retrieve his car in multiples of 30 minutes, the time required for one complete cycle.

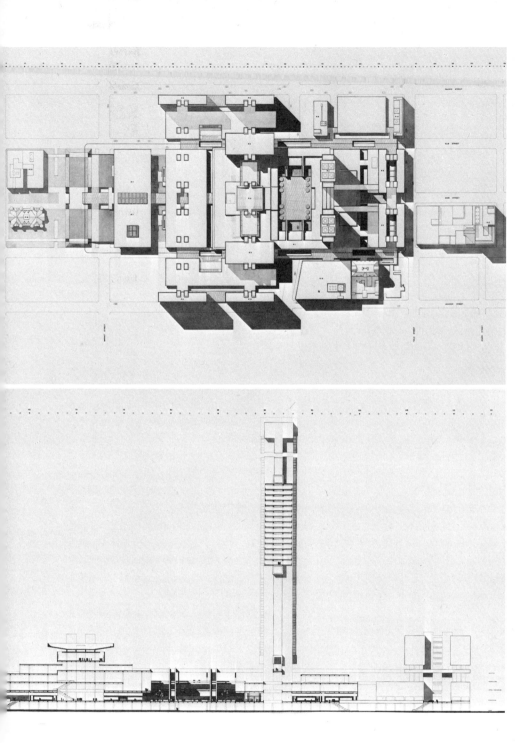

Like all utopian schemes, this one also claims collateral advantages —greater foundation capabilities for supporting the skyscrapers above on the walls of the pits, tapping of water for the city, storage and purification of water by using earth strata, and use of the pits as public fallout shelters. The inherent disadvantages of this concept are obvious: dependence on a completely mechanical system that in case of power failure would make 680 automobiles inoperational, and also creation of a catalytic generator of traffic in the very heart of the urban core.

The concept of the use of the automobile in urban centers and subcenters has become so ingrained that, however ludicrous and illogical, it dies rather hard. Equally so is the preoccupation with the use of gadgets in relieving traffic congestion rather than in attacking the core of the problem—the use of the automobile itself. The costs of continuing the use of private automobiles for intraurban central-space travel are not only financial; they are also human in that they prevent the logical shaping of urban spaces and are a potential health hazard. An international conference in Strasbourg in 1964 pinpointed air pollution from automobile engines as a cause of lung cancer and other diseases. In fiscal terms air pollution costs many millions annually, and is still higher in terms of health, productivity, esthetics, and the enjoyment of urban life. The concept of an all-electric automobile as an answer to urban air pollution is presently being studied as an alternate to the combustion engine for urban service. The development of the all-electric car is presently hamstrung by the lack of sufficiently compact and light batteries, since the present designs are too bulky and too expensive for automobile use. Even if such a car is successfully developed, unless it is integrated into at least a partially automated system it will prove of no assistance in solving commuting problems.

In the postwar period many services have moved to secondary urban central spaces, and thus closer to home; therefore, travel to shop does not present the crucial problem that does the daily rush-hour traffic from the suburbs to places of employment of the urban centrum. Evening travel for cultural, recreational, and social reasons from homes to these dense urban cores also does not present the same problem because the number of travelers is far fewer and their time of travel is not so concentrated as that of the commuter.

Commuter transit to major urban hubs presents a problem for the whole emerging urban pattern of the megalopolis. It picks up individuals from residential streets dispersed over large areas, channels them into fast-flowing major arteries, and then dumps them at a central destination in tremendous numbers. No single transportation system is capable of performing this complicated, three-fold function efficiently. The automobile works rather well as a collector on residential streets, becomes wasteful in the transit corridor, and is an impossible encumbrance at the point of destination. The "park-and-ride" system, used rather successfully in Europe because of the more dense residential build-up around the core of the city, has proven of far less value in megalopolitan sprawl conditions. Since the public transportation system—the major ingredient of the "park-and-ride" system—in megalopolitan centers is still in its infancy, many innovations are possible that may in the future adapt this method to American conditions.

There is still some interest in the monorail train as the answer to fast public transit because of the adaptability of its construction to existing conditions, its elimination of the need of expensive rights-of-way, and its unique characteristics of being superimposable over street patterns and between, around, and over buildings. There is little advantage in speed or passenger-carrying capabilities inherent in the monorail system over the underground system. The imposition of the monorail system on already formless, confused, and chaotic central urban areas would be little improvement over the ugly overhead expressways and place a final

*An early sketch of a proposed station for the Washington subway system, a
use of space which assists little in dramatizing computerized commuter travel.*

mark of "uglification" upon the face of central spaces. The monorail system is best suited as a secondary transportation system between centers and subcenters set in a harmonious macrolandscape environment.

The underground system, too long delayed in a majority of megalopolitan urban centers, is today extremely expensive to construct because of the heavily built-up central areas and the expansive suburbs it would have to serve. For these reasons most transportation planning concepts attempt to utilize to the maximum the potential of existing streets.

A system of automated bus trains capable of operating on residential streets in individual units, and then combining on the expressways into fully automated trains capable of high speeds, is in the developmental stage. The Chicago Transit Authority has been conducting preliminary tests that have proven successful and is continuing this study. The advantages of this system over the "hard" rail type are its flexibility, quiet operation, and ability to use existing streets, and also the fact that it is particularly adaptable as the collector of local traffic in suburban sprawl conditions.

Intraurban central-spaces transportation has the most intimate and direct impact upon the function and form of the urban heart. Once the passengers have been discharged from rail or other rapid transit at grade-separated central terminals, whose downtown distribution capacities are high, the problem of creating a satisfactory, human physical environment of the center-city begins. Even assuming the eventual total ban of the private automobile from the urban core, the problem of separation of pedestrian movement from public vehicular movement will remain.

Almost all the new concepts in the planning of central urban spaces recognize this problem and propose various remedies, which in one form or another depend upon maximum separation of pedestrian movement from any vehicle circulation within the urban core. Victor Gruen's concept for Fort Worth, Texas, depends upon all-underground tunnel truck deliveries and huge parking garages surrounding the downtown area. This concept, besides being extremely expensive, has other serious faults. In surrounding the core of the city with five huge parking garages, a Chinese wall is created that separates the center from the rest of the urban fabric—a rather antiseptic and foreign element in the over-all structure. This is further accentuated by the necessity to provide moving belts from parking areas and transit destinations and for overreliance upon private automobile transportation to the center, making the development spread out to impracticable dimensions.[1]

To date there have not been developed urban-design solutions on a city-wide scale that are based upon a balanced circulation system consisting of the various available new modes of intracity transportation—for example, moving sidewalks, new types of escalators and elevators, fully automated and semiautomated intracity transit—all of which totally

[1] Frederick Gutheim, "Urban Space and Urban Design," *Cities and Space,* ed. Lowdon Wingo (Baltimore: Johns Hopkins University Press, 1963).

integrate buildings with transportation and circulation patterns into a signficant form.

## 2.  THE SEARCH FOR FORM-COHERENCE

The shaping of a vibrant urban environment depends greatly upon the imagination, skill, and vision of the urban designer. The complete integration of the multitude of functions and activities within the central area into a well-orchestrated whole depends upon the subtlety, strength, and conceptual ability of the designer.

The challenge inherent in the search for form-coherence is illustrated in recent thoughts on harnessing the growth dynamics of the Washington metropolitan area. Among the alternate designs discussed by the National Capital Planning Commission in "A Plan for the Year 2000" was one generally based on a multitude of central urban spaces dispersed over the whole metropolitan area, a concept that accepted the existing pattern of urban sprawl and attempted to work out designs for central areas within these conditions. Since this theory of metropolitan planning would mean a continuance of the present pattern of development, it would be the easiest to implement as it would require no changes in existing policies. The new residential developments would continue to consist of single-family housing, and the planning controls would be limited basically to planning new, small urban subcenters. High-density development would be limited to the existing centrum of Washington and the area surrounding this hard core. This concept would be based almost entirely on private-automobile transportation. Each small central urban space would fall more or less at the intersection of the diagonal grid, which would form the basic structural order of the urban fabric. Between the internal peaks of density around the subcenters would be small zones

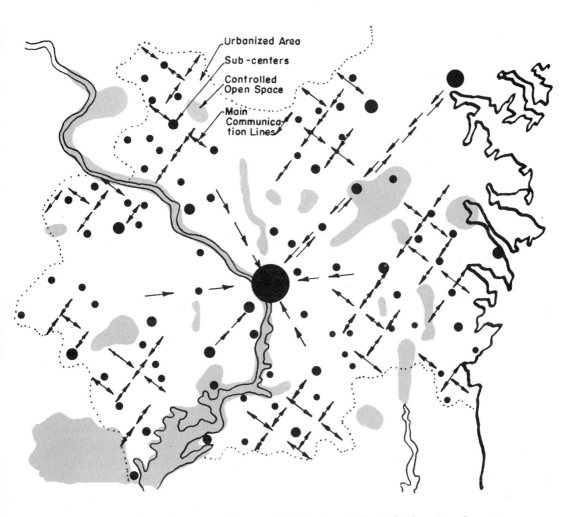

Study of planned metropolitan sprawl. National Capital Planning Commission, "A Plan for the Year 2000."

of very low density or entirely open land—thus providing open country-side within 10 to 20 miles of the center. This concept accepts long automobile travel, and within this plan public rapid transit would be of little use.

In this design the town center would contain shopping centers, some employment, and occasional apartments. This galaxy of small central urban spaces would largely negate much of metropolitan and megalopolitan advantages, and severely limit the opportunities for the choice of modes of travel, employment, social contacts—highly prized items of the urban American, who wants a great spectrum of choice in these matters.

The largest area served by each subcenter would be limited to no more than 100,000 people, and not every subcenter would be identical. A special effort would be made to provide for maximum variety within this controlled, planned sprawl. This concept is bound to receive a great deal of public support, since it follows the traditional, "natural" path of least resistance and recognizes the romantic and basically rural notions of private house, private lot, and private automobile—still very close to the heart of most Americans.

This scheme, heavily new-urban-center oriented, offers a challenging opportunity for shaping many small central urban spaces but little for reshaping the old ones—the basic foundation of megalopolitan development.

An alternate concept would be to increase greatly the density of the existing hub of Washington along the lines of mid-Manhattan and, while increasing the concentration of the old centrum, to construct a ring of new urban hubs on the periphery of the metropolitan area, along the 30-mile radius from the old hard core. While the metropolitan center could in this scheme solidify into a generally vertical form, capable of rock-type living for millions of people in extremely dense and concen-

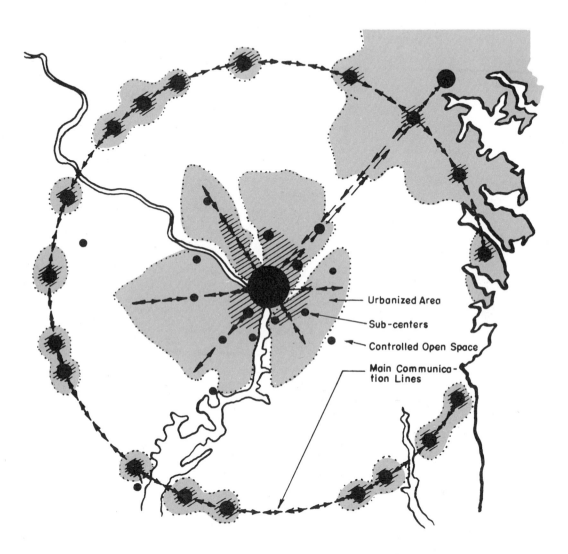

Labels within figure:
Urbanized Area
Sub-centers
Controlled Open Space
Main Communica-
tion Lines

*Study of a ring of cities. NCPC Year 2000 Plan.*

trated conditions, the cities along the perimeter would be shaped anew with desirable densities, functions, and forms. The area between the vertical space and the more horizontal peripheral galaxy of new centers would be divided by an open green belt, which would serve to contain and control the spread of the core as well as of the rim.

Transportation within the ring of cities would be via a circular rapid rail and rubber transit, both public and private, and the connection with the skyscraping hub would be provided by means of transportation spokes. This rigid and utopian concept is too static to contribute towards solving the problems resulting from the dynamics of urbanization and in shaping significant megalopolitan urban central spaces. Besides, governmental and legal controls necessary to implement this rigid scheme would be so cumbersome that the idea would stand little chance of being effectuated.

This concept is based on the assumption that offices, communal facilities, residential dwelling units, and related services would be totally integrated in the core into a vertical unit; the new peripheral development would be equally self-sufficient; and their mutual relationship would be only across open space, across time, and across greenery. As such, this concept seems to be the very antithesis of megalopolitan structural trends, growth patterns, and inherent potential.

Many versions of the above concept have been proposed for megalopolitan hubs. They vary from new peripheral communities to be built along the immediate edge of present suburban developments—an adaptation of the planned and controlled sprawl idea—to versions of freer, less form-connected, and dispersed satellite cities. Although more realistic in selecting sites for new city centers on the basis of topography or other practical considerations, this latter concept, based upon the English concept of new satellite towns, particularly of the London metropolitan region, does not recognize the existing patterns of development of the megalopolis.

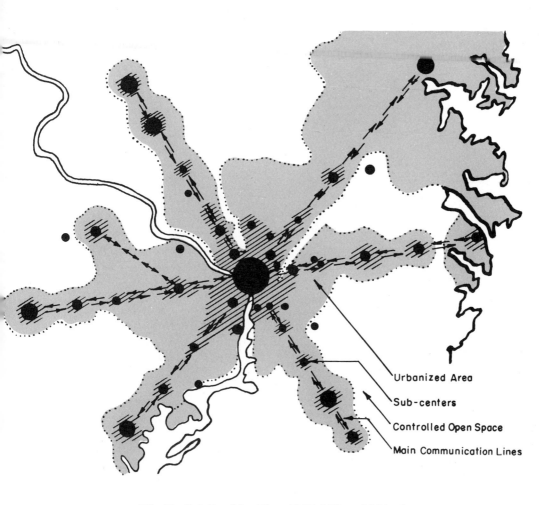

Urbanized Area

Sub-centers

Controlled Open Space

Main Communication Lines

*The Radial Corridor Plan. NCPC Year 2000 Plan.*

Among the concepts developed and proposed as a general guide for shaping and controlling the growth of megalopolitan hubs, the regional development plan for Washington for the Year 2000 appears to recognize the principal issues of megalopolitan development of central urban spaces and to come closest to providing a general framework for guiding and shaping their growth. It is based on an urban configuration resembling the form of a six-pointed star, with its centroid the old centrum of the city.

Unlike the concepts that envisage the upward, vertical development of the core into a mid-Manhattan type of development, this concept proposes comparatively little upward revision of the existing density pattern within and around the central core. It also prohibits suburban sprawl by limiting future expansion along radiating corridors. Although each of these is to be designed as a unit, to a large degree self-sufficient, with its own centers of employment, commerce, and housing, the main advantage of this concept lies in its adaptability to megalopolitan regional development.

One of the corridors, the northeast corridor, continues from the hub of Washington all the way to the very center of Baltimore, thus tying this metropolitan galaxy together and integrating it with the rest of the megalopolis. The flexibility of this concept allows it to preserve and utilize existing urban spaces and to tie in future ones along the regional transportation routes. The principal problem of this concept is that it contains the danger of being congested at the center and that movement from one corridor to another might be difficult. The circumferential highways, already constructed around this and other megalopolitan centers, will serve to provide circumferential movement, while the corridors will serve as the chief carrier of the voluminous traffic to the primary centers—the all-important urban cores.

Besides serving as an efficient collector of commuter traffic, intra- and interurban central-spaces transit, this concept presents the megalopolitan adaptation of containing urban development by means of green wedges, rather than by difficult-to-implement and growth-confining greenbelts. Since to date there has not been developed a total megalopolitan concept of an over-all macroform and fabric, this thought for the southernmost section of the megalopolis does provide an analysis of the changing functions of central urban spaces.

In this proposal the main transportation lines within the corridors are designed primarily for rapid mass transit. However, private auto-

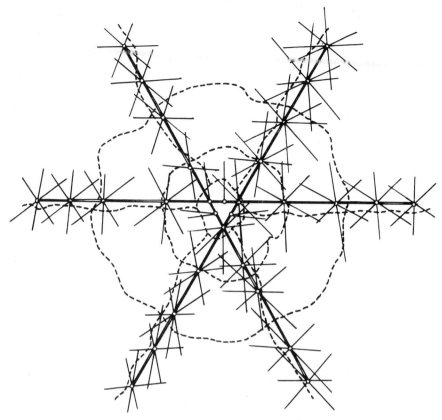

*An attempt to shape the emerging regional form. Rapid transit and freeway radials focusing on the metropolitan center, the latter supplemented with a ring of circumferentials. Plan based upon a balanced transportation system of mass transit and individual modes of travel. NCPC Year 2000 Plan.*

mobiles would also be integrated into these corridors, as the concept is based upon the assumption that all forms of transportation will be necessary for megalopolitan urban life. The main circumferentials are envisioned, on the other hand, as chiefly serving individual private motorcar travel, but here again the integration of a "soft" type of public transportation system is also possible.

This scheme proposes a maximum addition to the existing population of Washington of only a million people, mostly in newly organized central urban spaces within the presently urbanized metropolitan area. Future growth beyond the 3-million figure would be along the corridors and around new subcenters.

The hub of the new subcenter in this proposal would be located immediately adjoining the corridor spine, consisting of freeway, rapid transit, and arterial parallel roads, with "park-and-ride" stations located between these new satellite developments. The hub would be organized around a central transit station, with an adjoining employment center housed in towers facing a horizontal development of apartments and service buildings. On the opposite side of this development, high-rise apartment towers would be located, with the community's cultural activities as their nucleus. The remainder of the hard core of this new central urban space would consist of horizontal medium-density housing with integrated small service areas. On the opposite side of this hard core and across the transportation spine would be located small industrial parks, intensive and unobstructive in character. The extensive industrial areas would be located away from urban areas, on the fringes of green wedges.

Housing density within the hard core is envisioned in this concept as being around 80–100 dwelling units per acre, surrounded medium-density housing of 2–4 dwelling units per acre, the entire complex in turn surrounded by a low-density belt of 1 to 2 dwelling units per acre. This radial pattern would be interrupted by small greed wedges penetrating the housing belts as well as the hard core itself and connected with its center and interconnected with other nuclear units along the corridor by means of radiating residential arteries. Neighborhood schools would be spotted throughout the housing belts in central locations and adjoining the park system created by green wedges.

The greatest and most significant impact of these regional concepts would be upon the form of the "old" centrum. Since all these thoughts are based upon the almost universal assumption of an efficient and highly concentrated mass rapid-transit system, the new arterial network and its terminal hub-transfer points would tend to affect significantly the shaping of the new form of the centrum.

## 3. PAST IS PROLOGUE

Places of employment in any white-collar capital will in the future predominate its centers and constitute its main function. Commercial cores of the "downtown" will assume a related, service-type character, and will tend to become integrated into the over-all fabric of employment, residential, and transportation complexes. Residential high-density developments within and immediately surrounding the hard core will tend to concentrate around the hub-transfer points of the key transportation system—an efficient circulation pattern together with proximity to employment centers to minimize house–work travel being one of the major objectives.

Since central urban spaces are undergoing a rapid change in function and form, attempts to deal with the forces of change in a limited degree only add further to confusion. For example, the almost total expulsion of dwellings, cultural activities, and human amenities, and the resulting turning of the centrum into an antiseptic, inhuman space, has happened largely unnoticed in this evolutionary process.

However, as the growth of central urban spaces is accelerated, this process does not make the original form of the urban fabric obsolete. The adaptability of some existing buildings to new functions and uses remains, and the over-all pattern and structure of regional development can be reconciled to megalopolitan conditions.

The roots of the design of the megalopolis are deeply imbedded in the creative accomplishments of the eighteenth and nineteenth centuries, and success in moulding a significant future urban environment depends upon the understanding of the basic pattern laid out in the past. Lack of understanding of the fundamental need for historic continuity and the inability to draw inspiration from a rich urban design heritage will fail to produce great urban culture. Spotty, disconnected, and superficial preservation of individual buildings in urban redevelopment areas will destroy the fabric of the environment and lead to mediocrity. Both sources of inspiration must be utilized in shaping truly significant central urban spaces: the rich heritage of the past and the challenges of new problems and new functions of the city.

Technoscientific progress, when matched with understanding, courage, and imagination, can in the hands of a creative urban designer be molded into a truly central and urbane human environment.

# VIII. THE CULTURAL RENAISSANCE: NEW FORMS AND SPACES

## 1. THE NEW SATELLITES

The redevelopment of malfunctioning and deteriorated central urban spaces has occupied the chief attention of planners during the postwar period, at the expense to some degree of planning entirely new centers and subcenters. Within the last few years, however, enough developmental work has been completed in this important field to be able to establish certain morphological trends in the design of new urban entities.

There are no plans at the present time to construct new major urban centers in the United States that, in size or importance, would compare with either such new and significant cities as Brazilia or Chandigarh abroad or the existing urban hubs of America. Rather, the trend is toward the creation of new towns and new spaces around some of the older cities. These new urban satellites, besides being a great design challenge, provide the opportunity of orderly regional development and assist in the process of organic decentralization. Thus, the location and the shaping of these new towns have a significant impact, directly as well as indirectly, upon the redevelopment of megalopolitan centers.

In the Washington metropolitan area a few such new communities are being planned. The first outstanding pioneering new town of the post-war period is Reston, Virginia, located approximately 20 miles away from Washington's urban core. Another example of a new town in the Washington-Baltimore area is the ably conceived and planned town of Columbia, Maryland.

Most of the limiting factors and political, legal, and professional boundaries that exist in the old cities and that often hamper their reshaping are largely nonexistent in planning new urban entities on open, un-

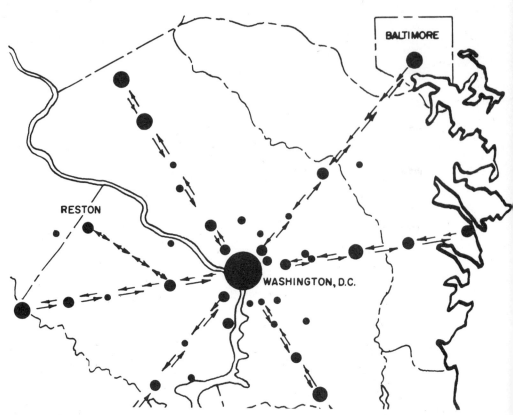

*Reston, Virginia.*

*The new town of Reston is being developed without government assistance, which is still not available for the planning and development of new communities. This first significant postwar satellite town in this country covers an area of 6,750 acres and is designed for a total population of some 75,000 people.*

developed land. Furthermore, right from the start these new urban spaces have the added advantage of having their location, function, and form determined to a large degree not by historical accident but by a planning process within an already established and functioning megalopolitan structure. Since these functions are inherently simpler than those of the amalgamated urban hub, their expression in physical form is clearer and more precise.

By limiting the total population of Reston to a relatively small com-

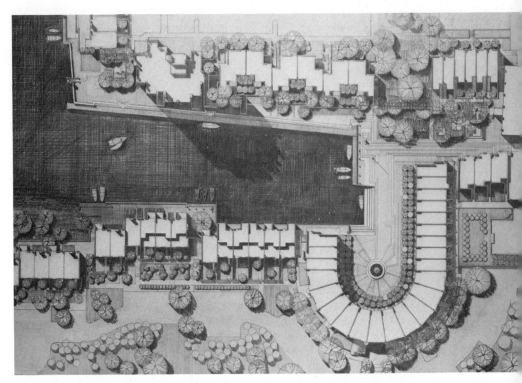

munity of 75,000 people, and given a well-defined transportation network, geophysical characteristics, and employment patterns, the form of the town and of its town and village centers results to a large degree from the skill and imagination of its designers.

The development of Reston and of its central areas is being planned within the existing regional pattern, and its chief aim is to provide an alternative to the postwar trend of uncontrolled suburban sprawl. Its location was determined almost entirely on the basis of transportation, the center of the town being near the intersection of two major highways: the recently completed outer circumferential expressway and the airport access highway between the centrum of Washington and the Dulles International Airport.

The major function of Reston is residential, that of a "bedroom" town, but unlike bedroom towns of the past—suburban sprawl in character—this new center will have a relatively high density, 60 people per acre in the "density sinews" that wind through the town, creating seven individual villages. Each of these villages will have a center containing

*Reston would not have been possible without new legislative measures that permit a higher proportion of space to be devoted to public use than is generally allowed in suburban sprawl areas; the amalgamation of commercial, residential, and recreational functions; integration of individual houses and townhouses with high-rise apartments; clustering of dwelling units and separation of vehicular and pedestrian circulation patterns. These legislative innovations were incorporated in a new zoning classification of the Fairfax County zoning ordinance, called the Residential Planned Community Zone.*

*Major central urban space—the proposed Reston town center.*

the following community facilities: a library, an art gallery, an auditorium, a church, some restaurants, and neighborhood stores with apartments above the shops. A conscious attempt was made to keep this "village" center as urbane in character as was possible on this small scale. The paved plaza around which central activities will take place contains a high-rise apartment. The presence of a lake front and large open spaces complete this idyllic scheme.

For those who do not enjoy "crowded" housing of 60 people per acre, ample, relatively expensive single-family housing is available with a density of under four per acre. These come with controls unique in America that restrict the design of the dwelling to a hitherto unknown degree. When completed, Reston's centers will offer to those who can afford it an escape from congested downtown environment and a real alternative to suburban living.

The contribution of Reston and of similar satellite towns can be

*The highly animated, vibrant, and integrated space offers a maximum of choice and reflects the excitement of a new central space. Both the first village and this study exemplify synoptic design.*

listed as follows: (1) They attempt to provide community facilities and recreational amenities within walking distance of the home to cut down the use of the private automobile. In a typical suburban community 30 percent of automobile trips are to work, 20 percent for shopping, 10 percent to school, 22 percent for recreational purposes, and the remainder for other reasons. (2) Located on major arterial routes leading to the great centers of employment, they facilitate efficient movement of people from home to work. (3) They attempt to provide its residents with a feeling of identity with a specific community and with an "urban" character that the suburban spaces of the megalopolis have so much lacked to date.

*High-rise apartments in Reston. Architects: Whittlesey and Conklin.*

*With legal tools designed to foster creative synoptic design, the planners and
architects were able to shape an environment that attempts to give meaning
to community life and an alternative to suburban sprawl.*

On the other hand, the inherent limitations of the new satellite towns in the image of Reston are equally significant. (1) If they follow the present pattern of development, these new towns will do relatively little in assisting to solve the mammoth social and economic problems of reshaping central urban spaces of the hard core—the real problem. (2) By being entirely privately financed and directed at middle- and high-income housing, this concept will not materially assist in improving the environment of the great urban hubs or raise materially the level of our urban culture. (3) The scale is small, when viewed from the standpoint of the dynamics of megalopolitanization, and the concept is rather precious and lacking in scope. (4) Designed without the guidance of the megalopolitan plan of development and without local historical continuity, there is the inherent danger that these towns may be conceived in a vacuum, thus becoming a conglomeration of novel architecture, passing and without much of a meaningful base.

The more recent design for the new town of Columbia, located in Maryland, in the Washington-Baltimore area, has attempted to overcome the lack of an established regional plan of development by making its own regional projections and then fitting its plans into these projected growth patterns. The planners of Columbia have also benefited from the experience of other new towns, and thus their plans express the most comprehensive, imaginative, and meaningful approach to shaping new satellite spaces of the megalopolis.

Columbia will consist of ten villages, widely varying in size, character, and form, each containing between 2,500 and 3,500 families and each with its own central space. These spaces will form the hearts of these communities and provide a wide choice of activities, amenities, and services. Each center, like each urban entity, will individually be designed in harmony with natural and man-made environment.

The focal point of each central space will be a village green, with scale reminiscent of the indigenous small towns of the Northeast. This

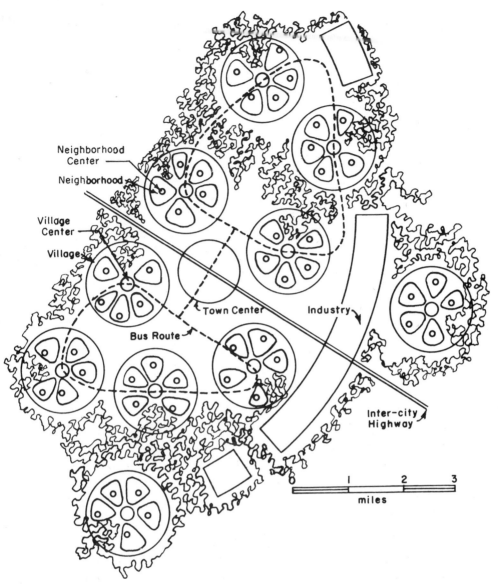

The design of the new city of Columbia, Maryland, exemplifies the synoptic philosophy as applied to the planning and shaping of a new community through a balanced appreciation of a hierarchy of values. In order to be a community, all social classes are housed and provided with cultural and educational amenities necessary for the refinement of social development and the evolution of culture.

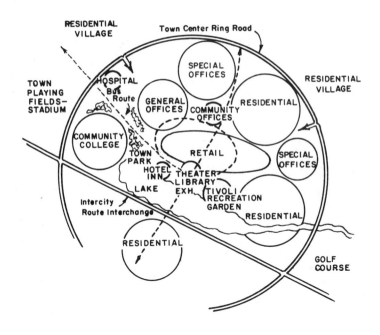

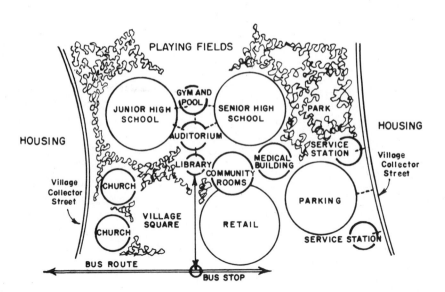

*Although only time will enable this new urban entity to become a city in the true sense of the word, the designers, fully aware of it, have done their utmost to provide enhancement toward the realization of this goal and objective.*

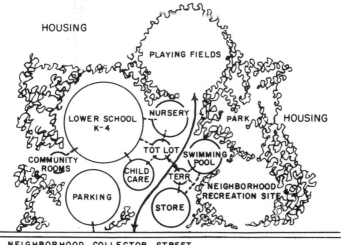

HOUSING PLAYING FIELDS HOUSING

LOWER SCHOOL K-4 · NURSERY · PARK · COMMUNITY ROOMS · TOT LOT · CHILD CARE · SWIMMING POOL · TERR · PARKING · STORE · NEIGHBORHOOD RECREATION SITE

NEIGHBORHOOD COLLECTOR STREET

*Also financed without government support, Columbia may be able to develop without being an excessive tax liability. To allow for orderly fiscal development, the entire 15,000 acres will be declared an Improvement District, thus cutting down the capital costs of the early and most expensive period of development. Common services will be paid for through long-term bonds; all building will be according to the plan.*

sensitively landscaped space will be defined by attractive service stores, community shops, branch library, churches, schools, and other community facilities.

Each of these entities will consist of five to six neighborhoods, each with 500 to 600 families. The neighborhood center will consist of an elementary school, nursery school, kindergarten, child-care center, neighborhood store, and neighborhood recreational facilities.

The heart of Columbia will consist of the central urban space of this complex, the town center. This urban center will contain office buildings, a large enclosed shopping mall, a theatre, several restaurants, and a transportation center—all basic ingredients of a meaningful urban center.

The total design of Columbia, its integration within an efficient regional and internal transportation system, some recognition of a historical cultural base, sensitive development of new land, and creation of a form expressive of the gamut of the hierarchy of spaces marks this experiment as a major contribution to the art and science of shaping new spaces of the megalopolis.

*Innovative legislative and planning tools employed in Columbia have allowed the shaping of a significant new tightly knit city with human scale and inspirational spaces.*

## 2. IMAGEABILITY AND IMAGINATION

The new structural order and a rather sophisticated pattern of highways and expressways, superimposed upon a hitherto shapeless, sprawling mass of the megalopolis, is beginning to give it a unique and more discernible form expressed by the emerging identity of the transportation network. The vertical, dense urban centers and subcenters abruptly flatten out at the edge of the core into rather characterless and formless housing belts. These spread concentrically and then begin to stretch out tentaclelike along major expressways. The significant transportation lines radiate from the centers of major urban cores and interconnect them into an integrated starlike pattern, further accentuated by the concentric rings of circumferential highways, that tend to pinpoint major central urban spaces. Such a megalopolitan air view of the structure of this urban phenomenon is, of course, not visible or even perceptible from the ground. The same constituent factors that from a bird's-eye view appear as connecting elements, from eye-level form barriers, chasms, and walls that disrupt and tend to fragmentize further the already amorphous urban spaces.

This dichotomy of imageability of megalopolitan form is also the result of the impact of urbanization—of new dimensions in the scale of urban areas. The speed of contemporary regional movement is exerting a form-giving influence upon the total organization of the megalopolis and an evermore meaningful impression upon its central urban spaces. This great urbanized region is developing a sensuous form, which can be given ultimate expression in the design of central urban space.

Urban design within this broad, magnificent, new scale is possible, but not in the stereotyped and presently static form. Looking back at the spiritually satisfying, often easily comprehensible town squares of the past, with a view to adapting these forms to modern urban hub dynamics, misses the real challenge of the intrinsic excitement and the animated dimension of central megalopolitan life. Planning wholly oriented towards solving problems of the present or reflecting the images of the past ignores the great challenge of megalopolitan life—fundamental opportunities of choice; great variety of urban environment; stimulating, enlightened, and dynamic culture.

The shaping and molding of central urban spaces as significant centers of urban culture in harmony with our cultural heritage is by far the most difficult and the most important problem facing the urban designer. Megalopolitan cores are already the centers of this region. However, under the impact of the forces of urbanization these spaces have tended to lose their original and all-important function as the center of community culture. The chaos, formlessness, confusion of modes of transportation and communication, poor accessibility, and other negative elements resulting from growth dynamics have been responsible for the almost total dissipation of this urban function.

During the daily working hours the streets and squares of the megalopolitan centrum are crowded with people and vehicles, with noise, movement, and life. At night, with the exception of such colorful central urban spaces as Times Square in Manhattan, most urban cores are deserted, unused and unsafe, and thus dehumanized. On Saturdays and Sundays there are no traffic bottlenecks, no crowds, few pedestrians, and almost no "problems." The urban Sunday life or the diverse evening activities of great cities like Paris, Rome, and London are rather limited in the American center. This cannot be explained by arguing that the spaces are not there to be used or that they are not designed for enjoyment, as almost every great centrum possesses a multitude of inviting and pleasant urban spaces. Washington is again a case in point, possessing extensive parks in the very heart of the city, many pleasant squares, and a great many urban spaces of unique character and interest. An important problem lies in the total physical separation of housing in suburbia from the central urban spaces, a condition creating a duality of functions not conducive to central, homogeneous cultural and social urban life. The megalopolitan man who spends an excessive amount of his time and energy during the working day in commuting is not prone to drive his automobile downtown again at night to spend his leisure time in an urban setting.

Backfeed of some housing to the heart of megalopolitan urban hubs, together with an efficient transportation system, will enrich the cultural potential of central environment and will assist in turning these hubs from ghost centers into the dynamic cores of urban civilization. The creation of a balanced, dignified, dynamic, and truly expressive megalopolitan central environment is the chief responsibility of the urban designer. To achieve such balance and harmony the present pattern of extreme competition and individualism carried to absurdity must be halted and a unified urban design frame superimposed.


## 3. THE FORM-GIVERS

New plans for such vital urban hubs as Washington, Baltimore, Philadelphia, Newark, New York, New Haven, Hartford, Boston, and Providence are beginning to indicate a hopeful common development trend towards reshaping central spaces as truly expressive of megalopolitan urban culture. The renewal of the center of the city is bringing the dynamics of urban university life and of its creative academic forces to play a new, intimate, and vital role in this cultural effort. Spearheading this movement, new to the traditional separation and aloofness of university life from community life, are the members of the university community—urban planners and designers. The researcher-designer and the practicing form-giver are brought into a close and intimate working relationship, particularly in the area of policy formulation and planning.

*An outstanding example of private development of central urban space com-*
*prehensively conceived is the New Town Center, a project which covers*
*approximately 105 acres of land in Prince Georges County, Maryland, near*
*Washington, D.C. Architect: Edward Durell Stone.*

*Twenty-six-story Knights of Columbus international headquarters, New Haven's tallest building. Designed by Kevin Roche of Eero Saarinen and Associates.*

*A mere decade ago stagnation and decay were destroying the vitality of New Haven's central urban spaces. The blighted conditions were reflected in an escape to suburbia, city maladministration, and a general feeling of hopelessness for the city's future. Redevelopment has already brought the city center from its doleful conditions to the threshold of building one of the most productive and human cities in the Northeast. Architect: Mies van der Rohe.*

The impact of these cultural forces upon the process of shaping central urban spaces is developing a truly great chain reaction and forms the mainstay of hope for the future cultural life of the megalopolis.

The last 20 years have revolutionized the practice of urban planning in the United States, and the presently evolving educational and research programs point to still further and more significant accomplishments. Many researchers and professors of urban planning and design are playing an increasingly more active and meaningful part in shaping central urban spaces in many multifaceted roles. The late President Kennedy's appointment of leading educators to national committees entrusted with shaping the central urban spaces of the nation's capital and the selection of world-renowned designers for important national projects points to a greater recognition of the role of the arts and the humanities in the design of urban environment. The establishment last year of national endowments and councils for the arts and the humanities should assist in encouraging leading artists and scholars to widen their spheres of activity and influence.

This rather new pattern of shaping central spaces by talented urban designers is breaking the tradition of center-city design by unimaginative individuals. It is also to a large degree responsible for the innovations, ideas, and new concepts of today and offers a hope for lowering existing legal, professional, and political barriers hamstringing urban design.

In eastern cities the trend of the ever-increasing influence of the creative designer and a greater cognizance of the basic processes of urban design on the part of leaders in government and business can be seen in significant accomplishments—utilization of the function and form of central urban spaces for maximum cultural and spiritual enjoyment.

The National Geographic Building in Washington designed by Edward Durell Stone is a dramatic example of a trend towards making office buildings the centers of cultural urban life as well. The entire first floor, set behind a recessed and landscaped arcade, is devoted to public

*Use of ground floors of public buildings for educational and cultural functions is one of our untapped urban resources. Interior of the National Geographic Society Headquarters, Washington, D.C. Architect: Edward Durell Stone.*

use, and this forms the integral extension of street and sidewalk life. The lighted interior of the ground floor is designed as a museum with exhibits of general interest that are housed behind huge glass enclosures, readily accessible to the public. In the middle of the exhibits is a large pool with lights and fountains transforming this space into a well-orchestrated urban environment conducive to relaxation.

Another design of the same architect, the proposed John F. Kennedy Center for the Performing Arts, which will be located in the midst of a newly redeveloped area, has stimulated a lively public discussion as to its role in achieving the objectives of the trend towards an ever-greater amalgamation and incorporation of cultural amenities with other functions of central urban life. The location and design of this building have

*Monumental expression of today's dynamics of cultural life is difficult to express through dignified, static forms and spaces. It is equally inappropriate to place these activities outside the heterogeneous central urban life. Spontaneous and gregarious cultural development will not be assisted by monumental, however dignified, solutions. The John F. Kennedy Center for the Performing Arts, Washington, D.C. Architect: Edward Durell Stone.*

severely been criticized for the limited utilization of this potential. Its alternative location on Pennsylvania Avenue would better have served this aim by integrating these great cultural functions into the core of the city.

Central sites for public buildings of nonmonumental scale and character are particularly suitable in and around central business areas. Locating these employment centers in direct and intimate contact with the business community expedites the daily contacts with other central urban activities. This trend towards placing public and semipublic buildings in the business city is another indication of the changing character of the function and form of office buildings, typifying the movement towards a total integration of all center-city activities.

The humanizing trend in shaping central urban spaces can be seen more in the all-important treatment of urban design details than in revolutionary over-all concepts. This is expressed in the design of small and intimate areas within the structures as well as without, and the creation of a multitude of transitional human-scale spaces designed to form the all-important link between the interior and exterior spaces of central urban areas.

Relatively small urban parks, parklets, and spaces designed for passive recreation, with benches, landscaping, and fountains, are recognized as important towards the creation of human environment in the megalopolitan centers. The practice of providing these all-important adjunct spaces as an integral part of any high-density private or public development is becoming more frequent.

Among predominantly residential central urban spaces of the nation's capital that pinpoint the search for an increasing expression of urban culture are two extreme examples: the first one the traditional Georgetown central urban space renewed by private efforts, and the other the new Southwest urban center redeveloped through government ac-

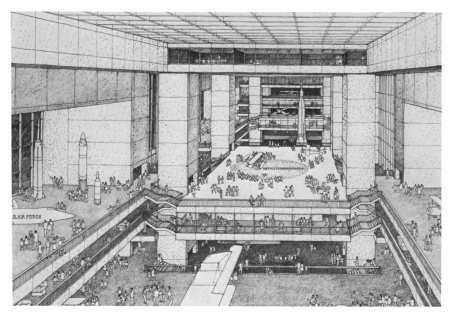

*A massive tribute to aerodynamics and man's conquest of air and outer space —an appropriate appurtenant structure to the temples of air transportation. Its internal space is dynamic and skillfully designed. This enormous space is expected to attract 5 million visitors annually. The character of this space was established by the decision to construct a forum containing almost 30,000 cubic feet in the center of the Nation's capital. National Air Museum, Washington, D.C. Architects: Hellmuth, Obata, and Kassabaum; and Mills, Petticord, and Mills.*

tion. Although these spaces are expressed in totally different form—the first one in traditional, psuedo colonial architectural mode, and the other in a form more expressive of the dynamics of today's urban life—they have an underlying, common basis of integrating some aspects of urban cultural life within an urban core residential neighborhood.

Georgetown, a horizontal central urban space consisting mainly of elegant Georgian and Victorian townhouses adjoining intimate open spaces and large parks, has succeeded in retaining the street pattern dating to the colonial era and in building upon a cultural foundation of the past by strongly restricting its development. Housing here intermarries with neighborhood shops, theatres, and other cultural functions into a homogeneous, if somewhat artificially preserved, central urban environment. The popularity of Georgetown as one of the most desirable areas of Washington, with the resultant exhorbitant prices of real estate, is a visible manifestation of the eager and total acceptance of such living conditions in the very center of megalopolitan cores. It also illustrates the need for a greater historical continuity in our urban development efforts.

The Southwest redevelopment central urban space, also located on the banks of the Potomac, is basically an apartment and townhouse complex, designed with rather extensive underground and ground-level parking facilities and with wide thoroughfares. The apartment towers are generously spaced, integrated with townhouses, and designed to provide maximum amenities. Commercial facilities are clearly adjunct in character, but the token cultural facilities do not suffice to form the spine and foundation of urban life that old Georgetown enjoys. The riverfront is being developed for recreation, promenade, boating, and fishing, and the small theatre is considered one of the outstanding examples of neighborhood theatres-in-the-round. This project illustrates the futility of attempting to design entire sections of a city in a cultural vacuum.

Regardless of the conscious effort that is made to humanize this space, this project generally lacks the essential intimate human scale, the significant open spaces, and the degree of integration of all central activities that are necessary for fully meaningful urban life. Only by total integration of urban functions through creative design, with human needs first and foremost in mind, can urban spaces be shaped into truly significant forms expressive of megalopolitan urban culture.

LEFT: *Civilization reflects the place of a people in history. The design for Pennsylvania Avenue is an intuitive expression of where we are as a nation.*
ABOVE: *The original plan for the National Square truly reflects through its New Empire-style the role in the world that we are still trying to discover. It is not the grand concept itself—which is to be admired—but the product which results that must be questioned. Its epic monumentality appears rather strange, foreign, and a little unconvincing.*

*Plan for Pennsylvania Avenue, Washington, D.C. The unabashed grandeur of the Avenue attempts to make it what it was not intended to be, never was, and may never be. There is perhaps too strong a relationship between the White House and the Capitol, with its lack of articulation and its regimentation. The greatest weakness of the plan is that it lacks cultural continuity. Every old building on that Avenue has an indigenous history. Cultural continuity is the continuation of creativity. The more we try to be monumental, the more we fail.*

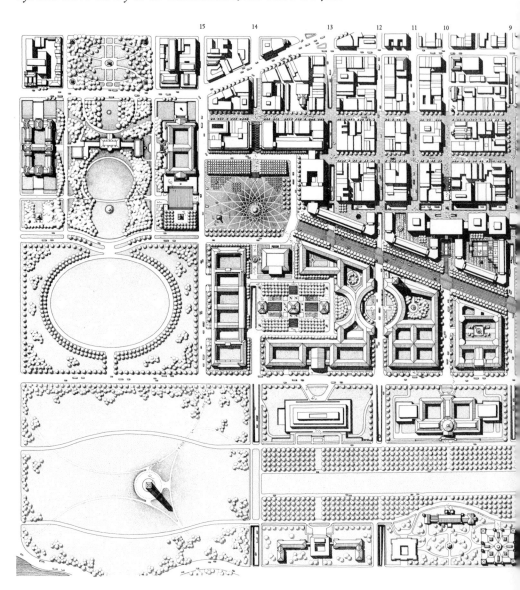

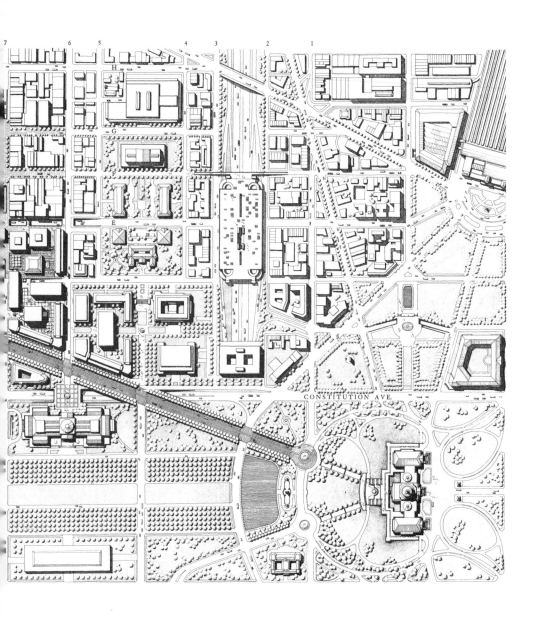

CONSTITUTION AVE.

*Final design of the culminating point of Pennsylvania Avenue—the scaled-down version of the National Square. Originally the National Square was proposed to cover an area of 800 by 900 feet. As finally approved, it will consist of a rectangular space 600 by 800 feet in area.*

# IX.  CONSPECTUS: TOWARD THE FULFILLMENT OF PROMISE

## 1.  THE NEW HIERARCHY

*The establishment of a new power structure for the megalopolis out of the existing operative units would constitute the formal declaration of purpose and intent of this unified region.*

Upon reviewing the evolution of the Northeast, many limitants to the logical and orderly process of shaping central urban spaces become apparent: planning is still suffering from two-dimensional land-use preoccupation; today's legal tools and the scope of present political boundaries are outdated and unsuitable to guiding urban development on a megalopolitan scale; both private and public activities have approached urban development in a compartmentalized manner, with emphasis on removing the blotches rather than recognizing the challenge of creating a new urban civilization; and the training of new leaders with technical skills and virtuosity in the arts and humanities is lacking.

The present pioneering and experimental nature of the renewal of urban hubs has shown the need for a coordinated effort aimed at developing the full potential of the megalopolis. The release of highly volatile and powerful forces into the streams of urban complexes without a synoptic design plan of development has proved to be wasteful and inadequate. With increased urbanization and the resultant complexities of urban life there are always dangers that these forces, when not adequately harnessed, may undermine the whole effort of urban development. There is no comprehensive instrument available today that could be used in measuring the elements of time, resources, and needs to assure comprehensive renewal and reshaping of central urban spaces in accordance with the changing urban functions. The multitude of sporadic and disconnected efforts, and the resulting overlapping and lack of long-term goals and appropriations, has given the renewal of urban centers a rather haphazard and introverted character. As Le Corbusier recommended for the reconstruction of France after the wartime deterioration and damage to its cities, "We must strive for the establishment of standards before we can approach the problem of perfection."

In order to develop adequate "standards" within the framework of a long-range development plan aimed at complete renewal of the central urban areas of the Northeast Megalopolis, existing governmental and professional boundaries should be extended to reach their ultimate potential. The governmental power structure within the Northeast Megalopolis does not reflect the changing function and form of this urban organism: the present hierarchy of city, county, and state governments should be adjusted to fit the existing urban pattern and to be in accord with future development objectives. The inability on the part of existing city governments to cope with the whole range of their problems is largely due to such limitations as inadequate powers to tax and control land and the often antique and meaningless boundaries inherited from the past. Planning on either a purely local or a regional scale under existing conditions must of necessity remain a piecemeal or academic exercise, a process inadequate to the task of the comprehensive development of an approximately 54,000 square-mile urbanized region.

The Northeast Megalopolis as an established urban entity ought to have some form of central body responsible for charting and planning its future growth and development. Such necessities as an efficient system of public transportation, comprehensive renewal of older urban centers, and the planning of new towns, public housing, and other social and economic programs should be placed within the jurisdiction of an over-all policy-planning administrative body.

Under a type of megalopolitan council system it would be possible to revitalize county governments, strengthen them, and thus provide a constituent body of megalopolitan government—the only practical approach since state boundaries divide the megalopolis. Many state constitutions presently favor the growth of individual municipalities at the expense of the counties. The expansion of governments of satellite cities and towns—already lacking resources, funds, and necessary services—should be discouraged. Instead, the urban county governments should be strengthened to become the all-important basic element of the megalopolis. Thus, this region—at present a conglomeration of weak, expensive, and ineffectual governments—could take advantage of the Supreme Court's principle of equal population districts to turn the urbanized county into a cohesive, powerful, and vital unit. The urban county is as representative of today's megalopolitan conditions as the city government and rural county were symbolic of the past. With the establishment of a new power structure for the region, and with a strengthening of already operative county governments, the upper limit of the government's ability to develop and control megalopolitan land in general and urban cores in particular may be reached. Since the majority of local municipal and county governments have long reached the pragmatic limits of their tax resources, which is particularly true in the densely urbanized Northeast, the federal tax system should be used to a much greater degree to form the financial base for the development of the megalopolis. The indebtedness of states and localities has since the end of the Second World War risen more than 60 times as fast as federal indebtedness. This is an indication of the costs involved in local development and the inadequacy of the property tax, which dates to the colonial era, as a tool for providing for greatly expanded and complex community services.

Since the end of the Second World War the acceptance of urban development as a national problem has increasingly been recognized through larger federal urban assistance programs, housing acts, and urban development acts, and finally the national Department of Housing and Urban Development. All of these measures have proven that the government recognizes the development of urban areas as a national problem. Similar attention to concerted action on a regional scale is now necessary. The recent concern for the large underdeveloped regional area of Appalachia should likewise be extended to charting the growth and solving the problems of one of the most developed areas—the Northeast Megalopolis.

At the present time presidentially appointed, fully empowered megalopolitan development councils, representative of all states and major centers of urbanized regions throughout the country, should be established. Each of these councils would be responsible for the policy formulation and development of a comprehensive plan for an entire region. These regions could well be the Southwest Pacific, Northwest, Gulf of Mexico, Florida, Piedmont, Ohio Valley, Great Lakes, and Northeast Atlantic.

In addition to these operative units there is need for the establishment under the President of an office of megalopolitan development that would coordinate action on the part of all agencies in the federal government responsible for urban programs—Department of Housing and Urban Development, Bureau of Public Roads, Office of Civil Defense, Office of Economic Opportunity being examples. Other types of action at other levels of government will, of course, be needed to accomplish this goal. Among the administrative reorganizations required one that is most apparent would be the realignment of regional offices of the new Department of Housing and Urban Development to make geographic regions conform to the level of regional development rather than to traditional geographic boundaries.

National defense considerations have, of course, played a vital role in placing local problems into a regional and national perspective. The National Defense Highway Act, the National Defense Education Act, and other measures point the way to a similar recognition of megalopolitan development in the context of national defense. Since transportation has already been recognized as constituting the skeletal structure of megalopolitan development and also of national defense, it will constitute a base upon which other programs—air pollution, water and power resources, shelter programs, etc.—can be approached on a regional scale.

The vitality of the constitutional system of the United States in adapting itself to change over almost two centuries of its existence offers a guarantee of its ability to encompass new ideas in the megalopolitan realm.

## 2. POLICY PLANNING

*The formulation of goals and ideals into definitive policy for the megalopolis and the preparation of an over-all plan for implementing this policy would constitute the immediate task of a Northeast development council.*

The renewal of urban America is an ambitious undertaking that will tax our capabilities to their extreme limits. This undertaking must go far beyond the scope of the present responsibilities of the Urban Renewal Administration. At the present rate of renewal more housing units are deteriorating into blight than are being renewed, and the efforts of the Urban Renewal Administration are hampered by inadequate and short-term budgetary appropriations.

The establishment of the Department of Housing and Urban Development in 1965 provided machinery to cope with urban problems on a national scale. In order to be successful as a national program, urban renewal activities in the United States will have to be recognized by the Congress as a primary area of concern. The members of Congress must be motivated to act for the renewal of urban centers as a national responsibility. This philosophy must be reflected in adequate and long-term Congressional appropriations for all urban development programs.

A major weakness of the urban renewal programs to date has been a tendency toward a division of power and fragmentation of authority both at the federal and the local levels. It is not surprising that federal aid administered through a multitude of assistance programs to thousands of areas in 50 states, over a relatively short span of time, has resulted in duplication and fragmentation.

The overemphasis on the "community," another major deficiency of these programs, has tended actually to encourage isolation of local government bodies by channeling federal aid to the "Local Planning Agency" and concentrating on the problems of small, individual urban entities at the expense of regional areas. In this way the Urban Renewal Administration was promoting a project approach, sometimes not in accord with the objectives of the Urban Planning Assistance Program, which recognizes metropolitan planning problems by giving assistance to metropolitan and regional planning agencies.

The lack of adequate coordination between the agencies administering various urban and regional federal programs is another major shortcoming of federal aid. This is particularly evident at the local level, where there is a proliferation of administrative units responsible for community development programs—urban renewal being administered by the local planning agency; comprehensive planning by the planning commission; housing programs by the public housing agency; and other programs by the office of the city engineer, welfare department, and numerous other constituent local bodies. Proper coordination between all federal urban programs would assure better community development, increase the speed of effectuation of all programs, and result in great savings.

In recent years there has been a significant recognition of the advantages of the rehabilitation of housing over actual clearance and redevelopment. This recognition is based upon findings that rehabilitation, whenever feasible, is more successful in terms of human, social, and architectural values and tends less to disrupt and break up both the existing fabric of the city and the city's historical continuity. At the same time, problems of family relocation caused by clearance operations are being studied, and relocation procedures are constantly being improved.

Although every effort should be made to rehabilitate what can be saved in the American community, many areas are deteriorated beyond the point where rehabilitation is justifiable economically or from the point of view of the city's over-all development, and thus the problem of relocation of families is becoming the number one challenge to urban renewal. Whenever a multitude of families are uprooted, a great number of human problems arise beyond those of mere housing.

Although the federal urban programs have stimulated planning activities at the municipal and state levels through the planning requirements that accompany these programs, these requirements have not in themselves been either stringent enough or comprehensive enough to assure well-coordinated development of the American community. In most cases these requirements tend to overemphasize functional and physical planning at the expense of comprehensive urban processes.

Among the various requirements of the urban renewal program is one that stipulates that the community possess a comprehensive plan of development.This is an example of how the great majority of federal urban programs that require planning on the part of communities and states before the granting of federal aid do so in a passive rather than a positive way. It is specified that the proposed projects be "not inconsistent" with existing comprehensive plans. Yet there is a marked lack of adequate standards that can be used in judging the "comprehensiveness" of these plans. And, in many cases, particularly in smaller cities and towns, such plans are extremely inadequate, not really comprehensive, and often outdated, but by the sheer fact of meeting the letter of the law the community is granted federal aid.

These basically administrative-technical shortcomings are, nonetheless, relatively easy to remedy even within the existing conditions. The more fundamental fault of this great innovative tool of urban development has been its use till now without broad enough and imaginative enough national purpose and intent, without adequate recognition of its ultimate potential as a tool for carrying out the ideas and principles developed two centuries ago on this continent. It has often blindly pumped vital forces into the mainstream of American urban life without recognizing the necessity of historical-cultural continuity of the areas that it aimed to renew. Thus, in order to unshackle the inertia of the recent past, during its initial years this tool has destroyed parts of America's cultural heritage. This may have been necessary in these experimental stages, but a nation on the road to developing a great urban civilization need no longer feel that in order to build the new it must destroy the old.

In order to develop the necessary criteria and standards for shaping primary and secondary central urban spaces, we must develop national policy as well as policy plans for all megalopolitan areas. In order to do this, the purpose and intent of our domestic programs have to be re-evaluated by the outstanding men of our time, a task requiring vision similar to that which the great leaders of the republic exhibited 200 years ago. These talents ought to be as available today as they were then, but they must be located and given the opportunity to develop a policy plan and a "balanced plan" of action aimed at cultural development as well as radical improvement of existing conditions.

Just as each local urban entity—the neighborhood, town, city, and county—needs a highly creative, comprehensive balanced plan for its orderly growth, it is that much more essential to develop a policy plan that would coordinate, guide, and give direction to urban development on a national and megalopolitan scale.

## 3. CULTURAL CONTINUITY

*The development of the megalopolis on the basis of existing foundations would constitute the clarification of our national purpose and intent in recognizing our urban heritage and using it as the source of inspiration of an evermore vital and purposeful development of our culture.*

In the search for solutions to the extremely complex daily problems of the burgeoning megalopolis, artistic and esthetic values are in the greatest danger of being entirely submerged by science and technology. This is in fact already happening, and therefore the humanities and arts must be given key roles in the development of urban regions.

The living history of cities is a unifying view of human values and accomplishments rather than a disjointed view of military feats or geographic movements of peoples. A study of the development of central urban spaces through history reveals the essence of the purpose and intent of each age. The development of our own central urban spaces, so full of meaning and significance, should be approached in this spirit. A city without a past is not a city—as evidenced by the inherent problems of such new, large urban developments as Brazilia or even our own new satellite towns. With the construction of new communities in the fringe areas, devoid of roots in the past, urban spaces in historic centers will become more meaningful. The tone, character, excitement, and vitality of some European cities are not the result of the greater ability of their planners and administrators to solve modern urban problems, such as traffic congestion and clearance of slums, but rather their ability through the centuries to build new and meaningful spaces through refinement rather than destruction of the old.

In this country there today exists a high degree of compartmentalization in solving urban problems, expressed in the competitive rather than complementary nature of programs of governments, the professions, and university disciplines. The disjointed quality of the national renewal effort, for example, can be seen in such areas as historic preservation: token financial and administrative interest at the federal level and on the local level almost a total misunderstanding of its inherent vital force. Living areas of cultural significance are often turned into wastelands or museum spaces containing individual buildings divorced from their context and thus robbed of their meaning. This reflects a lack of appreciation of what is significant and deserving of preservation and a misconception of what preservation is. The new, to be significant, must have its roots in the old.

In the past there was need for specialization and compartmentalization. The past 200 years constitute one of the greatest periods in the history of mankind, witnessing the rise of this continent from a subsistence way of life to a society of unparalleled affluence. But the continuation of the compartmentalization of a society in an affluent and developed stage is as wrong as would have been a purely synoptic approach to solving the problems of a subsistence society. In underdeveloped countries there is today a greater need for technical specialization than for philosophers and thinkers. In our own society there is a paramount need for philosophers, thinkers, and synoptic designers to give unity and cohesion to our cultural development. The skilled technician as such as a leader in society is becoming as obsolete as the worker in an automated industry.

Education for synoptic design must foster programs aimed at making man the master of technology and not its unthinking servant. Education today has two main faults: one is the inability to develop individual leadership qualities; the other is the inability to produce an individual whose skills and sensibilities are equally highly developed and refined. The training of synoptic designers must overcome these faults. It must, to begin with, attract the most vital minds and the type of creative individual that has in the past been drawn to the arts and the new horizons in the sciences. The synoptic designer needs an intimate grounding in the arts and humanities, a broad and deep substantive knowledge, and a thorough understanding of the processes of planning. He should possess the highest ability to develop technical skills as well as inborn intuitive design powers. In reference to synoptic design this means a simultaneous acquisition of pure and applied knowledge, fused together in a single harmonious entity. In the past there has not been enough recognition of the time and resources required to develop such an individual.

At the same time there is an equal need for full utilization of this talent, once developed. The existing reservoir of already well-trained professional cadres should be more fully tapped, and the future synoptic designers should have a vital role in urban development. The placing of a token number of talented planners, architects, and urban designers on a few advisory committees constitutes a wasteful use of the existing potential. New ways must be found to engage design talent in responsible working relationships in the vital stages of policy formulation, design, and implementation. Advisory commissions should be utilized not to work on insignificant details but instead as a source of creative ideas in the over-all design process.

The planning of the megalopolis and of its metropolitan areas must not be construed as a substitute for individual participation and local action in the creation and reshaping of urban spaces. The purpose of the over-all plan is simply to enable the development of a hierarchy of values and the clarification of purpose and intent for all major centers and subcenters.

Man's total environment must be construed not as the megalopolis, but as his immediate surroundings. The criteria of successful design must be based not only upon great, over-all, predominating thoughts but also upon the ability to see man as part of a great historical and cultural continuum and to shape his surroundings on a dignified, intimate, and human scale.

The essence of art lies in its ability not only to perceive truth but to express it in significant form and space.

# BIBLIOGRAPHY

THIS SELECTED LITERATURE is presented for reference purposes and is not intended to be all-inclusive. It does not include printed reports of governmental and private organizations that are cited in the text and can be obtained from the sources mentioned.

SYNOPTIC DESIGN

Burnham, Daniel H., and Bennett, Edward H. *Plan of Chicago,* ed. Charles Moore. Chicago: Commercial Club, 1909.

Cullen, Gordon. *Townscape.* New York: Reinhold, 1961.

Gibberd, Frederick. *Town Design.* London: The Architectural Press, 1953.

Giedion, Sigfried. *Space, Time and Architecture.* Cambridge: Harvard University Press, 1949.

Gropius, Walter. *Rebuilding Our Communities.* Chicago: Paul Theobald, 1945.

———. *The Scope of Total Architecture.* ("World Perspectives," Vol. III.) New York: Harper & Brothers, 1955.

Kepes, Gyorgy. *The New Landscape in Art and Science.* Chicago: Paul Theobald, 1956.

Le Corbusier. *Concerning Town Planning.* Translated by Clive Entwistle. New Haven: Yale University Press, 1948.

———. *The City of Tomorrow.* London: The Architectural Press, 1929.

Lynch, Kevin. *The Image of the City.* Cambridge: Technology Press and Harvard University Press, 1960.

Lynch, Kevin, Appleyard, and Myer. *The View from the Road.* Cambridge: Massachusetts Institute of Technology Press, 1965.

Scully, Vincent, Jr. *Louis I. Kahn.* New York: George Braziller, 1962.

Sitte, Camillo. *City Planning According to Artistic Principles.* New York: Random House, 1965.

Spreiregen, Paul. *Urban Design.* New York: McGraw-Hill, 1965.

Stein, Clarence S. *Toward New Towns for America.* New York: Reinhold, 1957.

Sullivan, Louis. *Kindergarten Chats.* Washington, D.C., 1934.

Tołwiński, Tadeusz. *Urbanistyka,* Vol. II, *Budowa miasta współczesnego.* Warsaw: Trzaska, Evert i Michalski, 1948.

Tunnard, Christopher, and Pushkarev, Boris. *Man-made America: Chaos or Control?* New Haven: Yale University Press, 1963.

Tunnard, Christopher, and Reed, Henry H. *American Skyline.* Boston: Houghton-Mifflin, 1955.

Wingo, Lowdon (ed.). *Cities and Space.* Baltimore: Johns Hopkins University Press, 1963.

Zucker, Paul. *The New Architecture and City Planning.* New York: Philosophical Library, Inc., 1944.

————. *Town and Square.* New York: Columbia University Press, 1959.

URBAN AND REGIONAL PLANNING

Abercrombie, Patrick. *Town and Country Planning.* London: Oxford University Press, 1959. (1st Edition, 1933.)

Abrams, Charles. *The City Is the Frontier.* New York: Harper, 1965.

Berry, J. L., and Pred, Allen. *Central Place Studies.* Philadelphia: Regional Science Research Institute, 1961.

Bogue, Donald J. *Metropolitan Growth and the Conversion of Land to Nonagricultural Uses,* Oxford, Ohio: Scripps Foundation for Research in Population Problems, 1956.

Carver, Humphrey. *Cities in the Suburbs.* Toronto: University of Toronto Press, 1962.

Chapin, F. Stuart, Jr. *Urban Land Use Planning.* New York: Harper & Brothers, 1957.

———— and Weiss. *Urban Growth Dynamics.* New York: Wiley, 1962.

Christaller, W. *Die zentralen Orte in Süddeutschland.* Jena, 1933.

Churchill, Henry. *The City Is the People.* New York: Harper & Hitchcock, 1945.

Clawson, Marion, et al. *Land for the Future*. Baltimore: Johns Hopkins University Press, 1960.

Dickinson, Robert E. *City, Region and Regionalism*. London: Oxford University Press, 1947.

Gallion, Arthur B. *The Urban Pattern*. Princeton, N.J.: D. Van Nostrand, 1963. (1st Edition, 1950.)

Geddes, Patrick. *Cities in Evolution*. London: Williams & Norgate, Ltd., 1949. (1st Edition, 1915.)

Gibbs, Jack P. (ed.). *Urban Research Methods*. Princeton, N.J.: D. Van Nostrand, 1961.

Gottman, Jean. *Megalopolis*. New York: Twentieth Century Fund, 1961.

————. *Economics, Esthetics and Ethics in Modern Urbanization*. New York: Twentieth Century Fund, 1962.

Haar, Charles M. *Land-Use Planning: A Casebook on the Use, Misuse, and Re-use of Urban Land*. Boston: Little-Brown, 1959.

Higbee, Edward C. *The Squeeze: Cities Without Space*. New York: Morrow, 1960.

Hilberseimer, Ludwig. *The New City*. Chicago: Paul Theobald, 1944.

————. *The Nature of Cities*. Chicago: Paul Theobald, 1955.

Howard, Ebenezer. *Garden Cities of Tomorrow*. London, 1902. (1st Edition: *Tomorrow*. London, 1898.)

Isard, Walter. *Location and Space Economy*. New York: John Wiley, 1956.

Jacobs, Jane. *The Death and Life of Great American Cities*. New York: Random House, 1961.

Lewis, H. M. *Planning the Modern City*. New York: John Wiley, 1965.

Lösch, A. *The Economics of Location*. Translated by W. H. Woglon. New Haven: Yale University Press, 1954.

Meyerson, Martin; Terrett, Barbara; and Wheaton, William. *Housing, People and Cities*. New York: McGraw-Hill, 1962.

Mumford, Lewis. *The Story of the Utopias*. New York: Viking Press, 1962.

Perloff, Harvey S. *Education for Planning: City, State and Regional*. Baltimore: Johns Hopkins University Press, 1957.

———— et al. *Regions, Resources and Economic Growth*. Baltimore: Johns Hopkins University Press, 1960.

Reichow, H. B. *Organische Städtebaukunst.* Braunschweig, Berlin, Hamburg: B. I. Georg Westerman Verlag, 1948.

Rodwin, Lloyd (ed.). *The Future Metropolis.* New York: George Braziller, 1961.

Saarinen, Eliel. *The City—Its Growth, Its Decay, Its Future.* New York: Reinhold, 1943.

Sert, José. *Can Our Cities Survive?* Cambridge: Harvard University Press, 1942.

Sharpe, Thomas. *Town and Countryside: Some Aspects of Urban and Rural Development.* London: Oxford University Press, 1937.

Tołwiński, Tadeusz. *Urbanistyka,* Vol. III, *Zieleń w urbanistyce.* Warsaw: Państwowe Wydawnictwo Naukowe, 1963.

Tunnard, Christopher. *City of Man.* New York: Charles Scribner's Sons, 1953.

———. "America's Super-Cities," *Harper's Magazine,* August 1958. 1299.

Tyrwhitt, J.; Sert, J. L.; and Rogers, E. N. (ed.). *The Heart of the City.* New York: Pellegrini and Cudahy, 1952.

Unwin, Raymond. *Town Planning in Practice.* London, 1909.

Von Eckhardt, Wolf. *Challenge of Megalopolis.* New York: Twentieth Century Fund, 1964.

Walker, R. A. *The Planning Function in Urban Government.* Chicago: University of Chicago Press, 1941.

Webster, Donald H. *Urban Planning and Municipal Public Policy.* New York: Harper, 1958.

RENEWAL AND DEVELOPMENT

Abrams, Charles. *The Future of Housing.* New York: Harper & Brothers, 1946.

Bogue, Donald J. *Population Growth in Standard Metropolitan Areas, 1900–1950.* Washington, D.C.: Housing and Home Finance Agency, 1953.

Capp, K. W. *The Social Costs of Private Enterprise*. Cambridge: Harvard University Press, 1950.

Colean, Miles L. *Renewing Our Cities*. New York: Twentieth Century Fund, 1953.

Conant, Bryant. *Slums and Suburbs*. New York: McGraw-Hill, 1961.

Dahl, Robert A. *Who Governs? Democracy and Power in an American City*. New Haven: Yale University Press, 1961.

Dyckman, John W., and Isaacs, Reginald R. *Capital Requirements for Urban Development and Renewal*. New York: McGraw-Hill, 1961.

Fiser, Webb S. *Mastery of the Metropolis*. Englewood Cliffs, N.J.: Prentice-Hall, 1962.

Fisher, Robert M. *Twenty Years of Public Housing*. New York: Harper, 1959.

Futterman, Robert N. *The Future of Our Cities*. New York: Doubleday, 1961.

Grebler, Leo. *Urban Renewal in European Countries: Its Emergence and Potentials*. Philadelphia: University of Pennsylvania Press, 1964.

Greer, S. *Governing the Metropolis*. New York: John Wiley, 1965.

————. *Metropolitics: A Study of Political Culture*. New York: John Wiley, 1965.

Hallenbeck, Wilbur C. *American Urban Communities*. New York: Harper & Brothers, 1951.

Landsberg, Hans N.; Fischman, Leonard L.; and Fischer, Joseph L. *Resources in America's Future: Patterns of Requirements and Availabilities, 1960–2000*. Baltimore: Johns Hopkins University Press, 1963.

McKenzie, R. D. *The Metropolitan Community*. New York: McGraw-Hill, 1933.

Riis, Jacob. *How the Other Half Lives*. New York: Charles Scribner's Sons, 1934. (1st Edition, 1890.)

Segoe, Ladislas. *Local Planning Administration*. Chicago: International City Managers' Association, 1941, Revised ed., 1948.

Straus, Nathan. *Two-Thirds of a Nation*. New York: Alfred A. Knopf, 1952.

Van Huyck, Alfred P., and Hornung, Jack. *The Citizens Guide to Urban Re-*

*newal.* West Trenton, New Jersey: Chandler-Davis Publishing Company, 1962.

Woodbury, Coleman (ed.). *Urban Redevelopment: Problems and Practices.* Chicago: University of Chicago Press, 1953.

————. *The Future of Cities and Urban Redevelopment.* Chicago: The University of Chicago Press, 1953.


TRANSPORTATION

Berry, Donald S. *The Technology of Urban Transportation.* Northwestern University Press, 1963.

Buckley, James C. "Comprehensive Transportation and Terminal Planning for Large Urban Centers," *Journal of the American Institute of Planners,* Winter 1947.

Horwood, Edgar M., and Boyce, Ronald R. *Studies of the Central Business District and Urban Freeway Development.* Seattle: University of Washington Press, 1959.

National Research Council. *Transportation Design Considerations.* Washington, D.C., 1961.

Owen, Wilfred. *The Metropolitan Transportation Problem.* Washington, D.C.: Brookings Institution, 1956.

————. *Cities in the Motor Age.* New York: Viking Press, 1959.

Ritter, Paul. *Planning for Man and Motor.* New York: Macmillan Company, 1964.

Smith, Wilbur, and Associates. *Future Highways and Urban Growth.* The Automobile Manufacturers Association, 1961.

Urban Land Institute. *The New Highways: Challenge to the Metropolitan Region.* (Technical Bulletin No. 31.) Washington, D. C., 1957.

Voorhees, A. M. (ed.). "Land Use and Traffic Models," *Journal of the American Institute of Planners,* May 1959.

Wingo, Lowdon, Jr. *Transportation and Urban Land.* Washington, D.C.: Resources for the Future, 1961.

Colean, Miles, and Nash, William W. *Residential Rehabilitation: Private Profits and Purposes.* New York: McGraw-Hill, 1959.

Finley, David E. *History of the National Trust for Historic Preservation 1947–1963.* Washington, D.C.: National Trust for Historic Preservation, 1965.

Green, Constance L. *American Cities in the Growth of the Nation.* New York: John de Graff, 1957.

———. *Washington, Village and Capital, 1800–1878.* Princeton, N.J.: Princeton University Press, 1962.

———. *Washington—Capital City, 1879–1950.* Princeton, N.J.: Princeton University Press, 1963.

———. *The Rise of Urban America.* New York: Harper, 1965.

Jacobs, S. K. *Historic Preservation in City Planning and Urban Renewal.* Washington, D.C.: National Trust for Historic Preservation, 1959.

Jones, Barclay Gibbs. *The Historic Monument in City Planning,* Society of Architectural Historians, Pacific Section, Spring Meeting. Eugene, Oregon, 1958.

Lees-Milne, James (ed.). *The National Trust: A Record of 50 Years' Achievement.* London: B. T. Batsford, 1946.

McKelvey, Blake. *The Urbanization of America, 1860–1915.* New Brunswick, N.J.: Rutgers University Press, 1963.

Morrison, Jacob H. *Historic Preservation Law.* New Orleans: Pelican Publishing Co., 1957.

Mumford, Lewis. *The City in History.* New York: Harcourt, Brace and Co., 1961.

———. *City Development.* New York: Harcourt, Brace and Co., 1945.

Olmsted, Frederick L. *Public Works and the Enlargement of Towns.* Cambridge, Massachusetts, 1870.

Providence City Plan Commission with the Providence Preservation Society and the Housing and Home Finance Agency. *College Hill: A Demonstration Study of Historical Area Renewal.* 1959.

Reps, John W. *The Making of Urban America*. Princeton, N.J.: Princeton University Press, 1965.

Tołwiński, Tadeusz. *Urbanistyka,* Vol. I, *Budowa miasta w przeszłości.* Warsaw: Trzaska, Evert i Michalski, 1947.


PROFESSIONAL JOURNALS

*Annals, American Academy of Political and Social Science*
*American Institute of Architects*
*American Institute of Planners*
*American Society of Landscape Architects*
*Architectural Forum*
*Architectural Record*
*National Trust for Historic Preservation*
*Progressive Architecture*
*Society of Architectural Historians*
*Traffic Quarterly*


FOREIGN JOURNALS
*Architectural Review*—London, England
*Australian Planning Institute Journal*—Sydney, Australia
*Journal of the Town Planning Institute*—London, England
*Kwartalnik Architektury i Urbanistyki*—Warsaw, Poland
*Town Planning Review*—London, England
*Urbanistica*—Turino, Italy

# INDEX

An italic number indicates the reference is in a figure caption or to a figure.

advisory committees in urban planning, 267
air-cushion train, *196–198*
Air Museum, National, *250*
airports: Dulles International, 163, *164–166*, 228; John F. Kennedy International, 163; Washington National, *162*
air pollution, 210, 261
air shuttle, 133
Alleghany County Port Authority, 201
American Institute of Architects, xii
American Institute of Planners, xii
Aristotle, 29
Attleboro, *132*
attraction potential, 8, 10, 11
automated bus trains, 212
automated highways, 204–*205*
automation, effect of, 14, 154
automated parking, *207–209*
automobiles, private, 52–57, 63, 128–133, 207–210, 232

balanced circulation system, 213
Baltimore, Maryland, 8, 19, 29, 33, *69*, 122, 138, 242
Bogue, Donald, 137
Boston, *5*, 11, 19, 29, *30*, 33, *86*, *87*, *95*, *96*, 122, 125, 131; plan of (1722), *30*
Boston Post Road, *34, 35*
Boutin, Bernard L., 110
Brazilia, 225, 265
Breuer, Marcel, 176
bridges: Memorial, 155; Theodore Roosevelt, *154, 155*; Verrazano Narrows, *145*
Broadway, New York City, *47, 204*
Brooklyn, New York, 33
Budd Company, 196
Bulfinch, Charles, 95
Burnham, Daniel H., 156
Bushnell Plaza (Hartford), *103*

Capital Beltway, *151*
Capitol Hill (Washington, D.C.), *114, 115*
Capitol, U.S., 172, *183*
Carnegie Institution of Washington, xii
Carver, Humphrey, 21
Census, U.S. Bureau of the, xii, 7, 38, 48, 54, 83
Chamber of Commerce of U.S., 106
Charles Center (Baltimore), *72*
Chicago Transit Authority, 212
circumferential highway, 131, *151*
Civil War, turning point in urbanization, 38, 40, 50, 62
civil rights, 84
classification of urban entities, 7–8
Colean, Miles, 71
Columbia, Maryland, 17, 234, *235–239*
Columbia Plaza (Washington, D.C.), 81
Columbia University, School of Architecture, 207
Commerce, U.S. Department of, xii, 55
Community Renewal Program, 76
commuting, 48, 122–135, 211, 220

comprehensive development regulations, 113

Congress, U.S., 26, 50–51, 67–68, 74, 81, 83–84, 261

Constitution Plaza (Hartford), *77*

Constitution, U.S., 33

control of building design, 93, 140, 170

conurbation, 8, 195

Cove Island Park, Stamford, *132*

creative federalism, 64–89

cultural continuity, 223–224, 234, 241, 265–268 (*see also* historic preservation)

Daft trolley, 48

Daley, Mayor Richard, 121

Dallas, 207–208, *208–209*

Davis, Alexander Jackson, *99*

density sinews, 228

Department of Housing and Urban Development headquarters, *176* (*see also* housing)

depression, impact of, 61–62, 65, 67

development of urban regions, 265

Dulles International Airport, 163, *164–166*, 228

Economic Associates (Washington, D.C.), 142

education for synoptic design, 266–267

electric automobile, *210*

electric trolley, *46, 49*

Emergency Relief and Reconstruction Act of 1932, 64

essence of art, 268

federal architecture, *114–115, 174–177*

Federal Housing Administration, 65

flexible formula, 86

Fordham University, Lincoln Square Campus, *66*

Fort Worth, 213

functional primacy, 11, 18

galaxy of urban spaces, 216

Gallion, Arthur, 65

Geddes, Patrick, 71, 91–92

general neighborhood renewal plans, 76

George Washington Memorial Parkway, 152, *153*

Georgetown, 138, 249–250

Goodman, Charles, 186

Gothic revival, 99

Gottmann, Jean, 8

Grand Central Station (New York City), 157, *161*

grants-in-aid, 73, 74

grid pattern, 42

Gruen, Victor, 213

Gutheim, Frederick, 213

Harral-Wheeler Mansion (Bridgeport), *99*

Hartford, xii, 11, 19, *77, 103*, 122

Harvard University, 33

Hellmuth, Obata, and Kassabaum, *250–251*

hierarchy of spaces, 237

highway,
 esthetics of, *109*, 147–155, 185
 role in urban growth, 57, 204–*205*

historic preservation, 88, *95, 99, 110–116, 119*, 223–224, 234, 263, 265–268

Historic Preservation, The National Trust for, xii

Holbrook, Stewart H., 40

Hoover, President Herbert, 60, 65

Housing Act of, The National: 1934, 65; 1937, 65, 67; 1949, 26, 64; 1954, 68, 71, 73; 1961, 64, 80, 81, 83; 1965, 64, 84, 86, 138

Housing Agency, The National, 67
Housing and Home Finance Agency, 61, 64
Housing and Urban Development, Department of, xii, 64, 75, 118, 176, 259, 260–261
Housing Authority, U.S., 65
Housing Corporation, The U.S., 52
Howard, Ebenezer, 91

immigration, 48, 60
Independence Mall (Philadelphia), 70
India Wharf (Boston), 95
Industrialization, effect of, 44

Jacobs, Jane, 18
Jefferson, Thomas, 33
Johnson, President Lyndon B., 84, 89

Kahn, Louis I., xii, 207
Kennedy, President John F., 81, 110, 247–248
Kennedy, John F., Airport (New York), 163
Kennedy, John F., Center for the Performing Arts, xii, 17, 247, 248
Keyes, Lethbridge, and Condon, 80–81
King's College, 33
Knights of Columbus headquarters, 244

Lafayette Square (Washington, D.C.), 111–113
Lanham Act, 67
Le Corbusier, 258
L'Enfant, Pierre Charles, 152, 172, 174, 192, 194
Lepawski, Albert, 23
Levin, Jack, 51
Library of Congress, 114–115

Lincoln Center of the Performing Arts (New York City) 16, 17, 66
Lincoln Memorial, 188
local indebtedness, 259
local planning agency, 262
Los Angelization, 166

Macadam road, first, 58
Main Place (Dallas), 208–209
Manhattan, 19, 37, 49, 116–117, 124–125, 143, 220, 241
Market East Study (Philadelphia), 202–203
Mass Transportation Program, 80
McKelvey, Blake, 44
megalopolis (see Northeast Megalopolis)
megalopolitan
    centrum, 241
    complexes in the U.S., 8
    council system, 258
    development councils, 260
    power structure, 258–260
    regional development, 225–239
Memorial Bridge (Washington, D.C.), 155
Meridian Hill Park (Washington, D.C.), 179
metropolitan planning agencies, 75
metropolitan sprawl, 215
Mills, Petticord, and Mills, 250–251
monorail train, 211
Mount Vernon, 191
Mumford, Lewis, 10, 102, 104

National Airport (Washington, D.C.), 162–163
National Capital Planning Commission, 124, 214–221
national defense, 260

National Geographic Society building, 246–*247*

National Square (Washington, D.C.), *253*

national urban policy, 261–264

Negro: families displaced, 120; housing, 50; and urban population growth, 60, 138

Newark, 11, 20, 122

New Haven, 11, *85,* 122, 207, 242, 245

New Town Center (Prince Georges County), *243*

new towns, 225–239

New York, City of, *2,* 10, 29, 32, 33, *45, 47, 49,* 50, 121, 122, 124, 125, 131, 138, *145,* 155, *198,* 242

New York-New Jersey Transportation Agency, 143

New York, plan of, *32*

New York Port Authority bus terminal, *15*

*New York Sun,* 52

nonresidential exception, 73

Northeast Megalopolis, 6, 8, 10, 14, 19, 29, 38, 54, 62, 84, 108, 122, *123,* 124, 195, 242, 257–260

Notre Dame, University of, xii

Oak Street Connector (New Haven), 85

Office of Megalopolitan Development, 260

Open-Space Land Program, 80, 88

park-and-ride, *132, 133,* 135, 211, 222

parking, *58,* 128–135, 197, 202–204, 207–209

Pawtucket, *126*

Pei, I. M., 103

Penn Center (Philadelphia), *78, 79*

Penn-Jersey Transportation Study, 204

Pennsylvania Avenue (Washington, D.C.), 249, *251–255*

Pennsylvania Station (New York), *116, 117*

Perkins and Will, *66, 96*

Philadelphia, *9,* 11, 14, 19, 29, 33, 50, 67, *70, 78–79, 82,* 110, 120, 122, 125, 138, 155, 197, *202, 203,* 207; plan of, *31*

Philadelphia, College of, 33

Philadelphia City Planning Commission, 197, *202, 203*

planning coordination, 262

Plato, 94

police power, 97

population growth, urban, 7, 23, *24–26, 39*

population of U.S., 1790–1960, *24–26, 39*

Population, Standard Metropolitan Statistical Areas, *123*

Providence, Rhode Island, 11, 14, 20, *109,* 122

Public Housing Administration, 86

Public Roads, U.S. Bureau of, xii, 55

Radial Corridor Plan, *219,* 220

railroads,
    effect of, on urban growth, 38, 42; era of, 40–43; of the Eastern U.S., 1840, *41;* terminals, *78, 158, 161*

rapid mass transit, 147, 195–204, *206,* 218–219

Rawlins Park (Washington, D.C.), *190*

Real Property Survey of 1935, 65

Reconstruction Finance Corporation, 64

redevelopment, urban, *5,* 64–89

regional planning agencies, 75

Reichow, H. B., 102

Reps, John W., 113

Reston, Virginia, 225–234
ring of cities, *217*
Riis, Jacob, 52
roads, *34–35, 57*
Roche, Kevin, *253*
Rock Creek Parkway (Washington, D.C.), 152
Rohe, Mies van der, *245*
Roosevelt, Theodore, Bridge, *154–155*
Rosslyn, Virginia, *171–173*
Rudolph, Paul, 207

Saarinen, Eero, 165, *253*
Saarinen, Eliel, 98, 101
Saint Louis Car Division, *196*
satellite communities, 225–239
Scully, Vincent, xii
Sitte, Camillo, 92–93
Slayton, William, 94, 104, 118
slums,
    investigation of, 1892, 51
    Washington, 182, *183–184*
Smith, Clothiel Woodward, 171
Smithsonian Institution, xii
Social consciousness, 62
Society Hill Towers (Philadelphia), *82, 119*
Southwest Redevelopment Area (Washington, D.C.), 20, 140, 192, 249, 251
Southwest, Tiber Island (Washington, D.C.), *80*
spatial form, 19–21
Stanley Brothers Steamer, *53*
Staten Island, 145
state planning agencies, 74
Stone, Edward Durrell, *243, 247, 248*
streetcars, *46–49*
suburban housing, 135–*136*
Substandard housing, 137, 138, 141
subway system, proposed for Washington,

D.C., *134,* 212
Supreme Court, U.S., 98, 259
synoptic design, 3, 28, 177, 266–268

Teletrans System, *206*
Tenement Housing Act of 1901, 51
Tiber Island, Southwest (Washington, D.C.), *80*
Toledo, 56
Tolwinski, Tadeusz, 101
traffic, *58–59, 65*
transportation: air shuttle, 127; private vs. public, 55; terminals, *15, 43, 133,* 147–166, 196–197, 202
truck transport, 54
Tube Transit, Inc., *199*
Tunnard, Christopher, xii

Union Square West (New York), *45*
Union Station (Washington, D.C.), 157, *158–160*
Unwin, Raymond, 91
urban county government, 259
urbanization, evolution of, 22, 29, 38, 61
urbanized area, 8, 83
Urban Planning Assistance Program, 74–76, 88, 262
Urban renewal, 61, 62, 68–83, 100, 104–121, 261–264

Verrazano Narrows Bridge (New York), *145*
veterans' housing, 50

Washington, George, 172, *191*
Washington, D.C., 11, 17, 20, 21, 56, 94, 98, *111–113,* 122, 124, 125, 128, 130, 134, 138–142, 147–194, 214, 216, 219–221, 225, 241–242, 246, *252–253,* 254–255; plan of, *36, 149*

Washington, The George, University, xii
Westinghouse Transit Expressway, *200–201*
White-collar revolution, 143
White House, The, *110–111*
Whittlesey and Conklin, *226–228*
Workable Program for Community Improvement, 71, 73

world urban centers, 10

Yale University, 33
Yale School of Art and Architecture, xi
Year 2000, Washington, D.C., 214–221

zoning, 71, 75, 88, 100, 113, 128–131, 140, 194